The Power of
Inner Peace

Other books by Diana Cooper:

Light Up Your Life
A Time for Transformation
Transform Your Life
A Little Light on Angels
A Little Light on Ascension
Golden Footsteps
(all Piatkus)

The following tapes by Diana Cooper are also available:

You Can Light Up Your Life
Discover how to create happiness, success, and health.

You Can Find The Right Partner
Learning exciting new techniques to attract the right person
into your life.

You Can Have Good Relationships
Change your perceptions and attitudes towards yourself and others.

You Can Take Wise Decisions
Learn to find your inner source of wise guidance.

You Can Overcome Your Fears
Understand your anxieties and phobias and learn to
overcome them.

You Can Find Inner Peace
Achieve inner calm and take control of all aspects of your life.

You Can Decode Your Dreams
Discover the purpose of your dreams and use them to solve
problems, meet a soul mate and help others.

You Can Enjoy Vibrant Health
Resolve the mental, emotional and spiritual factors underlying your
physical problems and regain health and vitality.

You Can Have Prosperity
Open to abundance and allow love, success and happiness to flow
into your life.

The Power of Inner Peace

Diana Cooper

PIATKUS

**To Gwendy, my aunt,
with love.**

*I would like to acknowledge the help and support
of many people, especially Lucinda Medd for her help
with the numerology and Grahame Freeland
for his unfailing encouragement and wise advice.*

© 1994 Diana Cooper

First published in 1994 by
Judy Piatkus (Publishers) Ltd
5 Windmill Street, London W1P 1HF

Reprinted 1995, 1997

This edition printed in 1998

The moral right of the author has been asserted

A catalogue record for this book is
available from the British Library

ISBN 0–7499–1948–5

Designed by Sue Ryall
Illustrations by Ken Leeder and Zena Flax

Set in 13/14.5 pt Monophoto Perpetua
by Datix International Limited, Bungay, Suffolk
Printed in Great Britain by
Butler & Tanner Ltd, Frome, Somerset

Contents

Contents

Introduction

We live in complex and changing times where many people feel insecure and powerless. I lived for many years with the chaos inside me of not knowing what life on Earth was all about, sensing there was some purpose but not really understanding it. When I was forty and at a time of total despair in my life, I had a spiritual experience which not only reminded me that there *was* a purpose to life but set me on a quest to seek the meaning of life.

Suddenly a new world opened up to me as teachers in all shapes and sizes came my way and reminded me of things I had always known. I 'remembered' that I was a spiritual being who had lived on Earth many times before. I knew that a higher aspect of my soul had chosen and carefully planned this lifetime because I had some tasks to do. I realized that I had decided to spend my early life paying off karmic debts accrued in other lifetimes. This meant that I had some difficult relationships and experiences to deal with. However, I knew that these experiences had strengthened me for the work ahead.

As I learnt that we create our lives on a moment by moment basis with our thoughts, words and actions, I realized that we may choose the chapter headings in the book of our life before we are born, but we write the chapters day by day and have immense power to change our lives. I wanted to transform my life and help others to learn how to transform theirs. Many of my learnings will be shared in this book.

One of the greatest comforts is to know that I never walk alone. I am surrounded by many spiritual guides and helpers who try to lift my spirits and show me the way. We all are. One of the greatest excitements for me was to find that I can open up and allow healing energy to flow through me to affect other people. I can also open up and allow higher information and wisdom to pour through me when I am speaking and writing. This is known as 'channelling'. We can all learn to do this if we want to.

Although I was brought up with a non-religious and non-spiritual background, I had always suspected that there was a God or Source or Divine Intelligence. After my original spiritual experience I knew it to be so. There is a Source, far beyond my comprehension, who is pure Love and who permeates all things. Only my ego self separates me from Source and I am constantly looking within to let go of my ego self in my desire to get closer.

When I claim my personal power, then I can be at peace. When I am at peace I have the strength to claim my power. It is a circle. Now I know that deep in my centre is a place of stillness and peace. From this space I can more easily access my higher guidance. Then I am empowered to do the Divine will.

I have come to understand that planet Earth is a school, a mystery school where our lessons are presented to us in the course of day-to-day living. Our tests and examinations are life's problems and challenges. Our rewards for good work are good fortune, joyous happenings and a sense of worth and wellbeing.

Once our soul is registered into the school of Earth, we return again and again. It is our Higher Self which chooses each incarnation for the greatest good of our soul. The choice is made with the help of discarnate spiritual advisers from an overall perspective of our soul's journey through many lifetimes. They will look at what experiences we still need, what aspects we need to strengthen, what karma we can reasonably repay or what service we can offer. Therefore everything and everyone in our lives is there because we have chosen them to be. Once we understand this and take responsibility for our lives, we gain a new awareness. We can then respond positively and grow.

Setbacks, challenges or difficult people may be a result of karmic debts we have accumulated in other lives and decided to repay in this life. Karma is the law of cause and effect. Whenever we do or think something which hurts or harms another, we owe it to them to put the consequences right. It becomes a debt. As you give, so you receive. We never get away with anything. Karmic debts are recorded in the account book of our soul. If we have pillaged a village in one life we may find ourselves drawn to rebuilding work in this one. If we have stolen something many lifetimes ago and not repaid, we will have something stolen from us.

Unresolved karma from past lives can cause us considerable pain. I trained as a hypnotherapist in order to be able to regress clients to re-experience or review incidents in their past lives which are still troubling them. They may need to exorcise a trauma, understand a situation or review events or relationships in order to heal something within their psyche, so that this life can be healthier or happier. Expressing repressed emotions starts the process of release, whereas understanding past events from a new perspective often helps people to forgive and to love again. Love dissolves karma. Karma is withholding love and love is for-giving.

I have also come to realize the importance of inner child and wise parenting work. Inside all of us is what is termed 'the inner child' – the immature part of us, the ego part, that struggles to feel safe, valued and loved. When we create in our imagination our own wise parents, who care for us and have our highest good at heart, we parent our inner child with love, encouragement and strength. As we listen to their voices of wisdom we start to live in peace and harmony, from which space we can make empowered and courageous choices.

I believe the creation of our own wise parents is an important and powerful way to self-healing and ultimately to mastery of our lives. When we are in constant communication with our wise parents within, we live at a raised level of consciousness aligned to our Higher Self.

Working with our chakras – our spiritual energy centres which act as transformers – also helps us to open up to our Higher Self. Learning to open, cleanse and strengthen these centres helps us to achieve wellbeing and spiritual growth and to open to Source. The work of the seven main chakras is described in this book.

When we have peace within we can more easily attune to the voice of our Higher Self. We can then access the knowledge, understanding and wisdom that our soul has acquired on its journey through many lifetimes. We also have an overall perspective of our life and that of others.

My hope is that this book will help you to develop and

maintain inner peace, whatever the outer circumstances of your life.

I wish you peace.

Diana Cooper

Workshops and Courses

Diana Cooper runs transformational workshops and courses in personal development and healing. For details, please write to her c/o Piatkus Books, 5 Windmill Street, London W1P 1HF.

CHAPTER 1

There is Hope

When life looks bleak, the spark of hope seems to be extinguished. The future appears as a burnt out fire, only a blanket of grey ash covering the skeleton of dead wood. Yet many such a fire has been fanned to life by an experienced hand with the bellows, so that within moments sparks and flames light up the darkness. So it is with our lives. We can learn to revitalize our inner spark and bring ourselves to peace and harmony again.

When nothing is going right

As Lizzie listened to the grey waves crashing onto the shore, she felt her own life was crashing in ruins around her. Everything had gone wrong. She felt bad and convinced that it was all her fault.

She had quarrelled with her partner and was sure he would leave her and go back to his old girlfriend. In her turmoil, she had bumped her car and was only covered for third party insurance. Worst of all she had worked day and night to prepare a project at work. She knew it was good –

much better than the others – and yet her boss had rejected it quite scathingly.

She stood huddled against the ice-cold wind, blaming herself, criticizing herself and putting herself down. Her thoughts went round in circles until she felt quite crushed, almost suicidal.

At that moment the sun glinted out from behind a cloud bank and she remembered one of our sessions. I had taught her to create wise parents, who could give her encouragement and advice at moments like these.

She stopped the negative selftalk and stood on the beach imagining her wise parents. Her wise nurturing mother said, 'You're hungry. Go and have a hot meal and you'll start to feel better. You know Jim loves you, so talk it over sensibly with him.'

Her wise father said, 'You've done really well, I'm proud of you. The project is superb, it deserves to be recognized. Your boss just doesn't understand your worth. It's time to be courageous. Go to see the Managing Director.' Then he added, 'Lizzie, you're beautiful, I love you. So does Jim.'

She listened to the wise voices and began to lift up her head. She left the cold beach to find a warm place to eat. Then, feeling much stronger, she went back to work and saw the Managing Director. He saw her point of view, liked her project and decided to overrule her boss. She felt empowered, validated and happy.

In that frame of mind, she went home and thought constructively about her difficulties with Jim. She could accept her part in creating them. When he came home she was warm, open and ready to be honest. They made up their quarrel painlessly.

Jim looked at the bump in her car. What had seemed

horrendous in the light of her negative mind set, looked little more than a small dent when she and Jim examined it. He said he could easily fill it and spray it for her.

When we listen to the voices of our wise parents, we see the world from a peaceful perspective. Lizzie went to bed that night feeling positive, peaceful and strong.

When we hold ourselves back

My friend Sue was driving out into the country for a weekend party. She felt happy, sexy and alive and looked forward to seeing her boyfriend. All of a sudden in her mind's eye she saw her father and stepmother, both long dead, sitting in the back of the car. Her father's voice was saying, 'You should be working not gadding about in the country, my girl.' She almost felt his bony fingers tap on her shoulder as he added, 'When I was your age we knew the meaning of work.' The sharp voice of her stepmother chipped in, 'Nice girls don't behave like that.' The voices whirled on with injunctions to stop enjoying herself.

Sue recognized those old familiar voices and for a moment felt the usual grey cloud of guilt and depression settle over her. But now she had new tools at her disposal. She shook herself firmly, mentally opened the back doors of the car and tipped out the carping, critical parents. Then she invited in her wise parents. They told her to have fun, reminded her she had been working hard and deserved a good break. It was time to let herself relax and really enjoy herself. She felt her spirits rise and started to sing. Her confidence and lightness returned. She had a wonderful weekend.

So many of us continue to let our moods be governed by

the negative injunctions of our parents. Their words remain as a record constantly playing in our heads long after they should have any parental control over us. Our parents cease to be our parents the moment we become aware of this. Then they become individuals with good and bad points. And they have no hold over us because we have started to parent ourselves.

The value of positive parenting

If parents bring up their child with wisdom and love, their child will have within a reservoir of inner peace. When we parent ourselves positively, we build our own pool of inner peace which no one can take away.

My work in teaching people to create wise parents to guide them has been born out of my own experience. I had a startling validation of this work when I had a spiritual reading from a well respected clairvoyant. A very powerful man came through for me. For a few moments she couldn't understand who he was. He was not a relative who had passed on, nor was he a spirit guide. Suddenly she said, 'How extraordinary: This is the father you have always wanted. He is strong and wise, he gives you inspiration. You created him yourself with your own thoughtforms, he is real for you.' She was impressed by the strength of what I had created. *And of course, we can all do it.*

What would your life have been like if you had had a fair, firm, supportive father who felt comfortable about being a man? Imagine if he had encouraged you, and showed he loved you.

If your mother had been wise and nurturing, if she had listened and understood you, if she had loved you and felt good about being a woman, how would your life have been?

But the truth is, no one has perfect parents. They simply do not exist on this planet, because we are here to learn and grow. When we recognize this we can begin to create our own wise parents. This means taking time to pause and ask ourselves, 'If I had perfect parents what would they be saying now?'

Wise people suspend criticism and judgement. They use encouragement, kindness and love to teach others. Our wise feminine voice may give us sensible, caring advice or simply remind us of our good qualities and gifts. Our wise masculine voice may give us strength and courage and help us to feel safe. These wise voices will always remind us of our link to the Source and the fact that the Power is within us so we can change our situation or our lives by changing our thought patterns. If we parent ourselves only with negative, critical, fearful voices we become depressed or anxious, powerless people.

When we parent ourselves with wise, loving, caring words we become immensely powerful. We can do anything and with this comes a feeling of inner peace.

CHAPTER 2

Parents as Teachers

Before we came into this life our soul chose our parents, our family and our circumstances. This choice was made with great care and with guidance from the spiritual advisers whose task it is to oversee our progress on Earth.

We understood then that our parents were the perfect people to teach us the lessons we needed to learn.

Re-examining now the reasons for those decisions can help us to comprehend clearly why we made those choices and what we still have to learn during this lifetime. This awareness, by changing our consciousness or mind set, can transform the way we view our life.

The value of tough lessons

If you want to become a champion jockey you go to the appropriate yard to train. Few become winners in their field without working very hard. They get knocked and bruised. They need total determination to succeed. A champion jockey has been well tried and tested on the way to the top.

When we want to evolve and learn about emotions and life on a physical plane, we choose to enrol in Earth School. Planet Earth is a training establishment in which life's challenges are our lessons. What we think of as a really difficult time in our life is a test we have chosen to take. It is an opportunity to learn, grow and become stronger. Those coincidences and surprise meetings are orchestrated by our Higher Selves to give us maximum opportunities.

Nothing we ever do, no experience we ever have, is wasted. When we do not learn from an experience, it comes back to us in some form, so that we have a chance to redo it. If we want to be a top-class jockey, we are not going to choose an easygoing, soft trainer. We choose someone who constantly stretches us. We may rail and complain but in our hearts we know it is the only way to accomplish what we want to. If we want to evolve, claim mastery and fulfil our spiritual destiny, we will choose relationships and circumstances which stretch us.

Dierdre had a mother who constantly pushed her. Whatever she did was never good enough, her mother always expected more. She felt bitterly resentful and hurt that what she could do was never acknowledged. Her father was elderly when he married her mother. Although he loved her mother, he was afraid of her and withdrew into his own world in the greenhouse. So he was never there to support Dierdre.

As an adult, Dierdre pushed herself beyond all limits. She undertook quite breathtakingly difficult tasks and pushed herself still further, yet she never acknowledged her own achievements. Continuing her childhood pattern, she attracted unsupportive men into her life. Her husband was weak and she had a series of unreliable bosses.

As she began to take responsibility for her life, she

realized that she chose her parents for teachers, just as a jockey chooses his trainer. When I asked her why she had chosen an unsupportive father and a pushing mother she had a burst of awareness. 'If it had not been for my mother I would never have achieved my potential,' she said. 'I would have been lazy and not tried.' 'And such a weak father?' I asked. 'If he had supported me, I would never have learnt to stand up for myself. I see I had to have a weak father, so that I grew independent.'

How we perceive our parents

We do not continue to treat ourselves as our parents treated us in childhood. *We continue to parent ourselves as we perceived our parents to treat us.*

When we are born our consciousness is the product of our past lives. We bring into this life all the beliefs we need to work on and these create our belief system or mind set. Even as a new baby or child, we translate everything our parents do or say according to our beliefs.

As we internalize those parental voices, they continue in our heads and become the voices of our inner parents. So in adulthood we parent ourselves as we believe we were parented.

If a newborn baby comes into this life with a belief in rejection, he may feel his mother is rejecting him if she leaves him with a neighbour while she goes shopping. If he wakes and cries he will believe that she is not there for him when he needs her and may feel devastated. The energy of this will be recorded in his unconscious mind. In adulthood when he feels needy, he will feel the same sense of devastation and will not know how to help himself.

We all filter everything our parents do and say through our beliefs and interpret accordingly.

When we incarnated we chose our parents because they were the right teachers for the lessons we needed. Their moods were exactly right to trigger the emotions we wished to explore. Their beliefs and fears exactly mirrored our own. Their life situation could satisfy our karmic destiny. They may well have been inadequate, hurting or even cruel. However, at a soul level they loved us so much that they became vehicles for our birth.

As we recognize this we can say to ourselves, 'I placed myself with these parents for a reason. What is it?' The sooner we understand why and learn the lesson, the more quickly we can move into a more comfortable space.

Authoritarian parents

If we found our father very authoritarian we need to look at the lesson he embodied for us. People are only authoritarian when they are very afraid of life. They think the outside world is dangerous and try to protect themselves and others with a rigid structure. If we had such a parent our life lesson is to face our fears.

Samantha's father was very critical and put her down a lot, so her life lesson was to learn to love and appreciate herself. The Universe constantly brought into her life people who criticized and devalued her. She knew it would continue to do so until she had changed something about herself.

She phoned me one day, sounding very upset. In a class she was teaching, one of the male participants was constantly criticizing her loudly and publicly. In the end, she

asked him to leave the class. He became rude and belliger-
ent and threatened to come the following week regardless
of what she said. She was terrified he would be there and
she wouldn't be able to handle it.

When she came to see me for an emergency session, she
was trembling. I asked her to close her eyes and go back to
the time when he was criticizing her and threatening to
come to the next class. With her eyes closed she could
feel the fear in her solar plexus and could connect it with
a feeling of not being good enough. This was a familiar
feeling from adolescence. She could pick out a time when
her father had said her exam results were disappointing
and she had the same devalued feeling. To her it felt like
crushing rejection. She told me she was afraid the class
members would feel she was a disappointment and would
reject her.

I asked her to create in her mind a fair, supportive
father who could encourage her and who would not stand
any nonsense from anyone. She saw the wise father she had
created come into her inner scene. He told her she was
O.K. and she heard him speak pleasantly but extremely
firmly to the critical man in her class. She felt an immediate sense of relief. I pointed out that this wise, firm father
was as much within her as the critical father and suggested
that she listen constantly to his wise voice.

She recognized that this difficult man had come into her
life to remind her of an unlearnt lesson. He was a test. She
knew that if she accepted she was good at her job, the man
wouldn't turn up. And if he did, she must be able to talk
to him calmly and firmly. So every day for the rest of the
week she closed her eyes and listened to the voice of her
own inner wise, fair and firm father. By the Thursday
evening she felt she could handle the situation whether the

man came to the class or not. He did not turn up so she clearly did not need the test. Her second validation was the fact that the class seemed to become more cohesive and supportive of her.

What Samantha now had was a tool to help her to deal with all the critical people in her life. As she used it constantly over the next few months, she became gentler and more loving towards herself. Her confidence grew and now she hardly ever gets criticized or put down. She simply doesn't attract those people into her life any more, nor does she automatically interpret comments as critical.

Controlling parents

Controlling parents, like authoritarian ones, are frightened inside. They try to control people or situations to make themselves feel safe. We have chosen those parents for our growth, so if we see them as controlling, we can assume that we too will continue to control ourselves and others in some way.

Some controls can be very subtle. If our mother threatened to leave us when we were naughty, we may have felt we had to be very good for fear she would carry out her threat. She may have controlled us with anger, withdrawal of love, threats of violence or emotional criticism. A hint here or there is enough to terrify a sensitive child. With a controlling parent, our lesson is to free ourself for no one can be truly happy in a cage and the illusion of bars cannot keep us safe.

John's mother died when he was a small child. She was never mentioned again within the family, because his father could not cope with his pain. The child believed he was somehow the cause of his mother's death and must be punished, so he kept creating accidents to hurt himself.

Within the family all emotions were suppressed. No one expressed their grief, their anger or fear at her death. In an attempt to keep control of the chaotic feelings he wasn't allowed to express, little John rationalized everything. He learnt to speak slowly and deliberately and spent his whole life protecting himself against the panic he dare not let himself feel. His father controlled the family in the only way he knew how, by denying his feelings. This withholds love. And there was the pervading threat of his anger simmering just under the surface.

John chose those parents for a complex mixture of reasons. For his mother to die when he was so young, John must have made a very difficult karmic choice before he was born into this life. It indicated that he had to learn to be independent, face his fears and at the same time to take care of his own nurturing needs. He also had to balance his own masculine and feminine energies without a mothering role model. Rationalizing, intellectualizing, being in the head, are a defence against feelings, so if we do this our personal mission is to get in touch with our emotions. John needed to do this. He also needed to free himself of inhibitions so that he could enjoy his life.

If we copy a very emotional parent our task is to recognize and master our feelings. Emotion is energy plus motion. Its purpose is to move us out from where we are stuck. If one of our parents is emotional and the other repressed, they both have the same underlying belief which is what drew them together originally. Perhaps their mutual belief is that they are unimportant. Underlying this is the feeling that someone who is unimportant is not worth staying with. So when this feeling is triggered, the emotional partner may respond with tearful clamours for reassurance, while the repressed one may become subtly controlling. They collude to handle their mutual fear of being left, which is the glue which keeps them stuck in the relationship.

Unsupportive parents

The bottom line of depression is feeling hopeless, powerless and giving up responsibility for ourself.

Kevin came to me with slight depression. He constantly cried, couldn't hold down a job and felt a failure. He still blamed his parents for his state. His father was distant and cool, his mother weak, selfish and a hypochondriac. Neither of them had been able to support him mentally or emotionally when he was a child. How could they? They used all their energy keeping themselves together. Now Kevin was in his late thirties and still constantly trying to get his needs met from his physical parents. He understood the concept of parenting himself but that meant taking responsibility for his own life — something he was far from ready to do.

When we choose weak, unsupportive parents our lesson is to find our inner strength, so we can support ourself. And if Kevin does not become strong enough to undertake this in this life, he will have to do it in the next one.

Don too had very little sense of worth. He was a relatively unsuccessful businessman who constantly worried about everything. I explained to him about the qualities of a wise mother and father. His response was, 'If I had a father like that I would be firmer with my employees and they would respect me. I would have the courage to go out and find new markets. Yes, if only my father had been like that, I know I could have been successful.' Then he fell into his customary role as helpless victim, 'but my Dad never encouraged me. He gave me no confidence.'

Don was in his forties. I pointed out to him that his father had parented him for perhaps fifteen years and he had been parenting himself for the past twenty-five years. What is more he had been parenting himself in the same way he felt his father had done. 'And now is your opportunity to change this,' I reminded him. He realized it was time to start to parent himself with an encouraging, strong, firm and helpful voice. The results in his business were quite startling. As he started to feel successful, he became successful.

When we stop blaming and take responsibility, we are powerful and at peace.

It can be very undermining to live with a critical parent in childhood. So why would anyone choose this experience? If we internalize our critical parent's voice, we will constantly have self-critical thoughts which can drive us to gloom, depression or even suicide.

We only take on board what fits our belief system. One child laughs at critical comments knowing them to be false. Another believes them and feels deeply wounded. If we hear the criticism, our mission is to learn to approve of ourself. To do this we must connect with our Divine essence. Every choice we make is to spur us on our journey to God.

Many people choose parents who seem to be total opposites. They may have a strong mother and weak father or an over-generous father and mean mother.

It is usually obvious that the weak partner leans on the strong one. However, the strong person is inherently weak and needs the weak partner to bolster his feelings of strength. This is why so many people who seem to be the strong supporter in a relationship disintegrate when the weak partner leaves or dies. If the person had been truly strong, he or she would have attracted in an equally strong partner in the first place.

The over-generous person and the mean one both have out-of-balance beliefs about money. Money is a love or power substitute. One is trying to buy more. The other is holding on for fear there will not be enough. The balance is a comfortable flow of giving and receiving. So when two people who live together express opposite polarities in this way, each has the same belief. We usually choose them as parents because we too hold the same underlying need to balance.

Where one parent is the villain and the other the hero they have colluded in the playing out of this scenario within the family. Both have the same lesson to learn. So if we think one parent is more at fault than the other, then our inner masculine and feminine will be out of balance. Our task is to get our picture of them into equilibrium.

If we imagine that our difficult parent has come especially to teach us a lesson, we can see our childhood differently. We can recognize that our parent may have loved us so deeply at a soul level that they were prepared to earn karma to help us learn what we so desperately wanted to.

It is no test to take on a thriving, well organized business. To test our business acumen we must bring round a business in difficulties. It is no test for an old soul, a soul who has been through many incarnations and is therefore quite evolved, to be born to wise loving parents. The real test of love comes in choosing parents who are damaged and to love them anyway. Most of us who choose damaged parents are undertaking difficult challenges.

Many amongst us are great souls, who understand this and can forgive and unconditionally love a violent, uncaring or abusive parent. And there are many more who become great souls as they patiently struggle with the lessons such a parent offers. When we succeed in mastering these most difficult lessons of Love, we become champions on Earth.

Forgiveness brings inner peace.

CHAPTER 3

First Lessons in Relationship

Our soul's energy is formed by the way we related to our past life experiences. So the consciousness we are born with contains the beliefs, awarenesses, knowledge and wisdom we have accumulated on our journey.

We constantly broadcast subliminal messages about our unconscious feelings and beliefs. At the same time we tune into other people's emissions. When we are seeking a relationship, whether it is a friend, a partner, a boss, or our parents before we are born, we will scan the airwaves to pick out those on the same wavelength. In this way we only attract people into our lives who match our unconscious patterns of belief and behaviour.

As the first people we relate to are our carefully chosen parents, we first learn about relationships from them. As a small baby or child we are sensitive to every nuance between them. With our delicate antennae we pick up all the tensions and feelings they try to hide. We also pick up their love and tenderness.

In whatever way they relate to each other, we have feelings about it. These feelings are what we have incarnated to experience. Whether happy or unhappy we will faithfully try to recreate them in our subsequent relationships. Where we have conflicting or unpleasant feelings, our mission is to try to resolve them. If we don't resolve them in childhood, we will attract or create similar relationships so that we can try again to resolve those same feelings. Many people spend a lifetime trying to get from someone else what they could not get from their parents in childhood.

Role models

As a little girl the first man who shows us attention is our father. He is our model of how we believe we deserve to be treated by a man. The little girl's mother is her first example of womanhood. If her mother feels unloved or uncared for as a partner, if she feels angry or abandoned or not accepted as a woman, the child receives frightening messages about the value of being a woman.

The small girl who senses that her mother feels safe and confident in her womanhood and who feels loved by her father receives a very positive message that it is good to be a woman. She is offered a solid platform on which to build her adult relationships.

In the same way, a little boy learns from his experience of his mother how he will be treated by members of the opposite sex. This is how he believes he deserves to be treated by women. His father shows him a role model of manhood and masculinity, which the child unconsciously copies. If the father is absent or emasculated or negative about life, the boy child may have a difficult time relating to himself as a man. If his father is confident and relaxed about his manhood, the boy learns it is all right to be a man.

The greatest thing we can do for our children is to untangle our own emotional problems so that we feel confident in ourselves.

Our belief systems

All emotions stem from our thoughts, which in turn come from our beliefs. We bring our beliefs into a new incarnation with us.

Our belief system is like a personal computer program. Any data presented to us that does not fit is ignored. If too much incoming information conflicts with our beliefs, we blow a fuse. We call it a mental breakdown.

Suppose we believe women are bad drivers. If we see a car accident involving a woman driver, we pick out evidence to support our belief it was the woman's fault, regardless of the truth. Our memory is selective. Countless people have sworn that they have seen or heard something and when presented with a video film or some contrary evidence, have found the truth unbelievable.

So we all interpret everything according to our computer program, our belief system. We see and hear selectively. We register things selectively. If we believe we are unlovable, we do not even register loving comments. If we believe we are ugly, we do not register compliments. If we believe we are a loser, we will 'forget' about the times when we have done well.

And of course the opposite is true. If we have a sense of self-worth we will not even register criticism aimed at us. It will float off us like water off the proverbial duck's back. If we know we are attractive we will not feel

25

diminished if a loved one admires someone else. If we feel successful, the times when we have failed will pale into insignificance in our minds.

Childhood relationships

In childhood we adopt a role in the family in order to survive. As an adult we continue to play out the role, and send out a powerful magnetic force which attracts someone who fits our pattern perfectly.

If Dad leaves the family when the children are young, a little boy may believe he must be the strong one and look after Mum. As an adult, he will continue to send out the vibration of that belief. He will then attract a partner who needs looking after or turn his partner into someone who needs to be cared for.

When Mark was seven his Dad abandoned the family leaving his mother with four small children to look after. As the eldest, Mark believed it was his job to be strong and look after Mum. As he grew older this was translated into, 'I must be strong and look after my wife.' Inevitably he attracted a woman who needed looking after. The patterns clicked.

He became aware of what he had done and when his first wife died he was determined to find a less dependent partner.

He married Tanya, a business woman who seemed very self-sufficient. But she had learned to fend for herself, because as a child she had never been able to rely on Dad. Underneath the self-sufficient exterior hid a little girl who wanted to be looked after.

Her little inner child felt safe and protected when she

was with Mark. She could let go of her self-sufficiency and lean on him. Before long Mark's pattern of being the strong, caring one was re-established. He took over her life and she became increasingly dependent. He turned the self-sufficient Tanya into someone who needed to be looked after, and they both unconsciously colluded to bring this about. At some level it suited them.

A small girl whose father has left home may believe that men will leave her. Then she will attract men with a pattern of leaving women or she will feel so insecure that she will push her partner into leaving. She may even avoid close relationships with men completely.

If a boy whose mother and sisters are busy and preoccupied has low self-esteem he may believe that women don't understand him and have no time for him. He is likely to attract a partner who is blocked and disinterested in him.

Take a little girl whose Mum is often sad or depressed. If she registers that Dad looks after Mum more solicitously when she is depressed, the chances are that the child will grow into a woman who becomes sad and depressed around men she fancies. Ultimately she will attract a partner who felt he had to look after his sad or sick parent. And she will reactivate his childhood feelings about his parent.

Roger was fatefully attracted to Wyn. In her teens she had had one bout of 'paralysis' and another of strange tingling sensations. Each episode had passed within a few weeks. When Roger married her she was a fit, healthy young woman. Within six months she was bedridden.

As a child Roger's mother was always ill. Roger would come home, shop, cook and clean, then read to her. He devoted his whole childhood to her. As a small boy and teenager he used to feel tears welling up at the sight of sick people and had a kind of precognition that he would always have to look after someone. Consciously he wanted to marry a robust, healthy woman but unconscious forces are much stronger.

Wyn's family was neglectful rather than abusive. She never felt loved, often felt alone and abandoned and learnt early that a headache was the best way of getting attention from Mum.

Throughout her marriage Wyn became increasingly ill. Roger took her from one healer or therapist to another but she never stayed to complete the treatment. Wyn came to see me twice. In the first session she passionately declared how much she wanted to be well for Roger's sake and how many people she had been to in her search for a cure. At one point she said the telling words, 'Of course, Roger will never leave me while I am so ill.' When I gently mirrored this back to her she became angry and defensive.

On her second visit she paused suddenly while she was in full flow about something else and said, almost as a throw away, 'I don't think our marriage would last if I got better.' Then she continued with what she was saying!

She never came back. Why should she? How could it possibly serve her? She needed to be ill in order to keep Roger with her. He needed her to be ill to fulfil a need in himself. They were colluding to keep the status quo. It was a sad, unhealthy and powerful pattern which kept them both locked in. A watered down version of this pattern is played out in many families.

If a child believes that she can never be good enough for Dad, she will probably draw a partner who puts her down. To feel not good enough for men, to be devalued is the norm for her. However uncomfortable, she is likely to seek out the familiarity of that feeling and only be interested in a partner who can give it to her. She will not be able to cope with a mutually valuing relationship. It will be too alien.

If a boy felt he could never please his mother however hard he tried, he will believe he's a bad person who can't make a woman happy. He is likely to attract a woman who is angry with men and nothing he can do will please her.

Annabel was a good-looking woman in her forties who had recently left her husband after many unhappy years. When I asked her about her childhood she told me her mother was absolutely wonderful. Her mother had been a pillar of strength and kept the family together. But her father, and her voice hardened, was a lazy, good-for-nothing. He couldn't earn enough to keep the household. He had hardly anything to do with the family, preferring to eat his meals alone upstairs in his room.

As she talked more about her childhood, it transpired that she would sometimes come home from school to find her mother gone. There would be a note to say she couldn't cope any longer. The house would be empty and Annabel would feel devastated. But she had to take care of the younger children. It was a shameful family secret and she never told anyone of her struggles. She bore it all *manfully*. Despite this she kept her mother on a pedestal and couldn't think anything bad about her.

When she grew up she was determined never to go through all that again. She intended to be in control of the finances and her children were never going to be faced with an empty house. She became the strong, controlling one.

She attracted an isolated man like her father. That

suited her well as she had never learnt to be close to a man. Her husband had a good job and seemed to be an excellent choice as a provider for her family. Of course, he had to also be weak enough to let her control him. She took over the family finances and disempowered her husband. She poured all her energy into looking after her children while her husband became more and more of an outsider. He became gloomy and quiet. He could never do anything right for her. No man could have done.

Eventually his confidence in himself foundered. He felt angry with her and wanted to punish her. Time after time he was made redundant or lost his job. What better way to get his own back without having to take conscious responsibility? With no regular income and a husband who was distant and unreliable as a provider, Annabel felt desperate. The children were leaving the nest and she was reconnecting with the devastated empty feeling she had as a child arriving home from school to find her mother gone. True to her mother's example she took the only course available to her mind set. She upped and left home.

If our feelings about our parents are out of balance, then our own masculine and feminine energy is automatically out of balance.

Annabel's healing started with the awareness that her mother had not been all that wonderful. She began to see that she had been controlling and rejecting and in some areas very weak. With this realization about her mother, she was ready to judge her father less harshly. She now saw that he was lonely and unhappy. She remembered how he spent hours trying to find work and when he came home his wife and children made him feel so pushed out that he ate alone. She recognized for the first time that he didn't want to eat alone. He just felt so bad about himself that he didn't feel he deserved to eat with the family.

The whole situation was a family collusion. Mother is wonderful and we must hide it from the world when she can't cope. Dad is bad and we must reject him.

As she unravelled the tangle of her family's patterns and her own, Annabel felt safer within herself. She was able to let go of the dominant controlling mother energy. She decided to remain separate from her husband and to learn to nourish and strengthen herself so that she could attract and create a more wholesome relationship next time.

There was no point in Annabel blaming her parents. They too were hurting and both the product of families with controlling, rejecting patterns. She knew that she had chosen her particular mother and father because of their patterns which she needed to experience in order to look at her own. Some of her life's lessons this time were to let go of control, learn to trust and open to love. She started a programme of parenting herself so lovingly and caringly that she began to feel at peace. Three years later she was living with a stronger, more loving and supportive man.

When we take responsibility for ourselves, it is our task to parent ourselves wisely in all our weak areas. Even relationships which are strong, supportive and working well on many levels can hold destructive patterns which act like cancers within the partnership if not recognized and dealt with.

Lisa ran a business where she never felt supported by her male colleagues. She realized that she was attracting weak men whom she did not trust to support her. She started to have conversations daily with her internalized wise father, and listened intently to his words of support and encouragement. Since that time she has always had at least one strong supportive man in her business life. It is as simple as that. The outer reflects the inner. When we recognize our patterns and parent our weak, hurting, sabotaging inner personalities constructively, we enrich our relationships.

Parenting our patterns wisely produces new choices and the possibility of deep peace.

CHAPTER 4

Understanding
Our Lessons

We have planned our individual tailor-made journey on this planet for a purpose. The route to our destination is flexible but we agree to stop at certain places to pick up pre-booked passengers and parcels. If we choose to take anyone else with us we may do so. We carry an illuminated sign which signals to everyone where we are going, whether we are on a fast or slow trip, exactly what sort of a driver we are and what baggage we carry. So whether it is for a short while or for the whole way we travel with people who have signed on to experience the journey with us. Nothing and no one is with us on the journey of our life by chance. We drive our own vehicle. We attract our fellow travellers. We choose what we intend to study on our travels and we have the freedom and power to book into all the places we want to visit in between the compulsory stops. While it is good to have a large scale local map, it is a good idea from time to time to look at a map which covers the whole route.

Life is not just a random set of circumstances over which we have no control. We are here to learn and have chosen our course of lessons so that we can grow. People often ask if it is necessary, or helpful even, to go back and look at our past lives to understand why we have chosen this life. I can only speak from personal experience. I have found it immensely valuable. It has given me a broad perspective of understanding – a complete picture that makes sense of the individual pieces of life's jigsaw puzzle. Relationship difficulties which can be so hard to heal in the perspective of one lifetime, make clear and obvious sense when seen over a series of lives.

Fears originating in past lives

Karen had always been an overprotective mother. She fussed over her daughter and treated her like a precious china doll. Her daughter found this claustrophobic and left home as soon as she could. Karen was upset and constantly worried about her capable daughter. Her relationship with her son was much freer and more wholesome.

It was only when she explored her past life relationship with her daughter that she understood what was happening. Karen had caused her daughter's death in a past life and she now made the connection that the disaster she feared would happen in the future had already happened. Now she no longer needed to fear it. She started to relax and enjoy a healthy relationship with her daughter.

Irrational fears become very understandable when the past life cause of the fear is revealed and frequently the fears then dissolve.

Molly always felt guilty and responsible if anything went

wrong in her family. There was no logical reason for it. Yet she often felt a kind of dread. When I asked her to go back to the source of the problem, she found herself as a young girl of ten in an oriental life. She had been sold as a concubine to a huge puffy man, who was very rich and powerful. When he tried to have sex with her, she was terrified and scratched his face with her long nails, causing him to lose face. The only way he could deal with this humiliation was to have her and her entire family slaughtered. She watched in agony as her entire family, including her young brothers and sisters, were put to death. Then she was left to die too.

As she looked at what had happened from the perspective of a different culture, she could see it was not her fault. She had only been a child. Just becoming aware of what had happened helped to lessen her feelings of guilt and dread. By bringing the episode to consciousness, her unconscious mind reinterpreted it and freed her.

Awareness frees us from the shackles of fear. Problems that we encounter feel less monumental when placed in the context of many lives, just as the setback on Monday is unimportant when the solution is found on Wednesday.

From three dimensions to five

Our soul has had many experiences on this and other planets and in other Universes before we came in for this life on Earth. Most of us bring in a complex tangle of conflicting beliefs and fears and want to learn our lessons now so that we can move up faster in Earth School and be ready for the changes ahead. Planet Earth is moving to a

Plane of Higher Consciousness where people live with unconditional love and take self-responsibility.

We are moving from a third-dimensional planet to a fifth-dimensional one (see Chapter 24) and those amongst us who are multi-dimensional are serving as bridges between Heaven and Earth. Many highly evolved souls are being born now to help this shift in consciousness take place.

The importance of Earth school is this: It is a mental, emotional and physical plane of experience where our inner thoughts and beliefs faithfully manifest, giving us constant feedback. Because it is one of the few schools in the Universe where we can experience emotions in a physical body, places here are highly sought after.

We have more opportunities for soul growth on Planet Earth than in any other plane of the Universe. And these opportunities are greater now than at any other time in history. We are called on to let go of fear and be counted as spiritual warriors. This is not always comfortable or easy.

Our unconscious invitations

We are all vibrational magnets. We attract towards us people and situations by the unconscious messages we give out. People behave towards us according to these messages. If we do not like the things that happen in our lives it is up to us to change our vibrations.

It is often quite easy to recognize in hindsight how we have made something happen.

James mentioned to me four times in the course of a conversation that he was sure someone he was working for would never pay him. If he was saying that to me, it is likely that he was also saying it to others and thinking it to himself.

Every thought we have, word we say and picture we see in our mind's eye is a message which is impressed into the Universal energy as something we want to happen. All of us are powerful creators of our own life.

James phoned me in fury six weeks later and said that the other man's firm had gone bankrupt and he wouldn't get paid for his work. He was quite aware of how he had created this and was angry with himself for doing so, but he had a tight empty feeling in his stomach every time he thought about it. He realized that he believed he didn't deserve to be paid and the Universe gave him exactly what he anticipated. He now wanted to change that belief.

He asked me to take him to the source of his belief and found himself in another life, poor, ragged and hungry. He and hanging onto it for fear he wouldn't get any more. He died of the effects of long-term malnutrition with a tight empty feeling in his stomach.

He then regressed into a life of opulence as a hard-hearted woman who allowed peasants to starve in a hard winter because she was too mean to share what she had. James half expected the first life but was shocked by the second one. I assured him that we have all done things out of fear in our lives and being too hard-hearted to share food with another is fear. The healing comes when we accept these aspects of ourselves and forgive them. Then we don't attract the same lessons to ourselves any more.

We are all immensely powerful and we use this power unconsciously to attract situations towards us.

Kate's father was in his nineties. He lived some distance away and needed nursing care, so Kate engaged a nurse who lived in and took care of him very lovingly. Kate grew very fond of her. When her father became more feeble and confined to his bed upstairs, the young nurse asked if she could have one or two things from the house for the flat she had bought. Kate agreed.

Although the nurse had not said so, Kate knew she was going to take a certain picture. 'I just knew it. I even saw her removing it in my mind's eye,' she said.

Months later the nurse was still devotedly caring for her father. Kate decided to give her various pieces of furniture which she knew her father would never see again and the nurse arranged for a friend to help her move them.

A few days later Kate visited her father and the picture was gone! She was furious. 'I knew it. I just knew it,' she said to herself. She calmed down and spoke to the nurse about it. The young nurse was genuinely upset and puzzled and thought her friend must have taken it thinking it was one of the items to be moved. Kate believed that the nurse was being totally honest, so she decided to meditate on it.

The message she received in meditation was that she was very powerful. Her thought that the picture would be removed had created its removal. She had sent the message into the Universe so clearly that the nurse's friend had picked it up and acted on it. She had removed the picture in all innocence thinking that was what she was supposed to do. *When we do decide to take responsibility for our creations we begin to realize how breathtakingly powerful we are.*

Years ago something similar happened to me. I didn't trust a man who gave me a cheque. It bounced and I was cross with myself for not listening to my intuition. I mentioned it to a friend and she said, 'Oh no. The cheque bounced because of your untrusting thoughts.' I knew in a blinding flash that she was right.

On another occasion I was on a tube train in London when it stopped at a platform and didn't start again. After some delay passengers were asked to continue their journey by bus. I was with two friends and we got out and stood on the platform in a huddle. One mused, 'Everything is a manifestation of Love. That means everyone on this train has a belief that Love can run out of power.' We decided that we had better change our belief and put power back into the train. The three of us stood on the platform and meditated on power. Within three minutes they had managed to restart the engine. Almost everyone had left by then but we got onto the train and continued our journey!

If something has happened we have made it happen or our energy has contributed to it happening. The only time we cancel out our power is when we send out mixed thoughts. That is when we get confusion in our lives. When we have two conflicting beliefs, the stronger manifests. To the extent that one is greater, that will appear in our life.

So if we believe we want a relationship but also believe that relationships cause pain, whichever belief is stronger will manifest. If our desire for a relationship is strong enough, we will allow a partner to come in but our other belief will also manifest and that relationship will cause us pain. If the second belief is stronger, then we won't even let ourselves have a relationship.

We nearly all have conflicting beliefs which is why our lives do not run smoothly. Our task is to weed out all the beliefs which no longer serve us. If we are an unevolved or unaware soul it may take a long time for our thoughts to work through into the physical. However as we advance up the spiritual ladder our thoughts will manifest immediately.

As we take responsibility for the power of our mind, which creates our life, we can harness this force for the highest good. Accepting this power and aligning it to the Divine Will brings a deep sense of inner peace.

39

CHAPTER 5

The Child Within

When our stuck child within wants to draw our attention to its predicament, it makes us feel discouraged, angry, shocked or out of sorts in some way. It may have a tantrum in part of our body, give us a migraine, tummy ache or make us feel sexually aroused. How else can it get us to notice its needs?

If we ignore its cry for help, our frantic child tries harder to attract our notice and most of us use a great deal of energy to disguise these uncomfortable and shameful feelings.

By talking to pain or to embarrassing or shameful thoughts and feelings as if they are a stuck child, we can start to reconnect with our needs and free our creative energy. We begin to blossom.

Putting on a good face

I saw a little girl of three fall over. She went down with a really nasty crash on her knees. She picked herself up and rubbed her little knees, saying aloud, 'Don't cry. You're not a baby.' I mentioned this to a friend who told me her neighbour's children had been taught to laugh – yes laugh – when they were hurt.

It is a short step from total denial of physical pain to denial of emotional pain. When we do this we can never be whole, in touch with our feelings, with genuine energy flowing through us. We will always have a dark, hurting hole in us. We don't realize that this dark hole is simply a bad feeling. We think we will be totally rejected if anyone sees our 'bad' side. There is a certain truth in this. If we act out bad feelings by raping, murdering, cheating and stealing, we will probably be locked away. If we translate them into jealous, bitter and carping words we are not likely to have many friends. However, we are mostly so frightened of our deep, dark feelings that we will not acknowledge them even to ourselves. Yet the more we lock away our secret feelings, the more they scream to be noticed and the more energy we use keeping them hidden. Then they run our lives. These feelings have power over us because we unconsciously fear we may act them out. We cannot feel at peace while trying to hide big chunks of ourself. When we accept and openly acknowledge our bad feelings, then the pressure is off and we can choose how to deal with them.

These darker feelings indicate unresolved issues we still need to work on. Often very outgoing, eternally cheerful people have a deep hurting or depressed space inside which they cover up at all costs.

Maria was bouncy, bubbly and bright, always positive and lifted everyone's spirits. She had a great energy to be around and was very popular. But when it came to working on her deeper, underlying feelings, she did not want to know. She said she thought there would not be any of her personality left if she did. Despite this resistance, another part of Maria wanted to look at her darker energies, wanted to clear them out and find peace of mind. As so often happens when we are ambivalent about progress, her Higher Self prompted her to look within.

A dream forced itself to the surface, a dream which dragged her down so much that when she talked about it during a workshop, the bouncy, bubbly, bright and positive Maria looked drawn and grey. Her eyes seemed hollow as she told it. I cannot remember the details of her dream now but I remember her drawing of it. She drew a tiny black figure curled up in a foetal position in a huge empty room. Her feelings were loneliness, emptiness, despair, abandonment and helplessness. For the first time ever she connected with these awful feelings. Until now she had held them back behind a huge walled dam. Now the wall was breached and the feelings seemed to engulf her.

The power of a workshop is the healing and support we can give one another. Maria was able to connect with and express her deepest fears. When she found that the group was willing and able to listen to her, understand her feelings and still respect and love her, something profound within her changed.

Over the course of a few days she returned several times to the deep, dark cave of loneliness and fear within. Each time she came back calmer and stronger. The group consistently held her both emotionally and physically and continued to love and respect her. It was a breathtaking revelation to Maria. She learnt that she did not have to hide her worst fears, that she would not fall to pieces if she admitted to those feelings, that people still loved her even though she was not consistently cheerful. Most of all she learnt that by accepting a part of herself that she had hated, she could turn the turbulent cave within into a well of inner peace. She remained bouncy, bubbly, bright and positive but it was now underpinned by underlying calm and self-acceptance.

Like all of us, Maria chose parents who were learning the same lessons. They too denied all feelings of depression or sadness and colluded to keep Maria's hurt, lonely, frightened part hidden. *When we accept all aspects of ourselves we have a clear, still pool of peace and tranquillity within.*

Underneath being nice

A very common pattern is for a girl to be considered unable to support herself. She is given a spoken or unspoken message that she needs a man to look after her financially.

This was certainly a very strong message in my family and I grew up believing I could not possibly earn a decent living. When I chose my first husband I knew I would be financially looked after. But, in exchange, I gave up emotional and creative independence.

Claire came from a very different background but she heard a similar message in her childhood. Her brother was given money and freedom but felt unnurtured and unloved. She was overprotected by both her parents, it was their way of showing love. She learnt that girls must be sugar and spice and all things nice so she became charming and pleasing. She absorbed the implied messages that girls could not look after themselves, and gave away her independence and individuality. She buried her anger and her jealousy of her brother's freedom and settled for a sheltered life.

Typically, she married a man who fitted into her family pattern. When they were first married she wanted to help her new husband with his business but he said, 'No, I want you at home.' She gave in. As her children grew older, she wanted to get a job but everyone disapproved. She gave in.

When she was forty Claire's husband found a younger woman who worked with him in his business and left her. The divorce gave Claire the shock she needed at a soul level to start a voyage of self-discovery. She became a counsellor. Not surprisingly her entire family, including her ex-husband, criticized and derided her work. There contiued to be a big family collusion to keep women financially powerless. Claire, however, was changing and was determined to stick to her new work. Her outward face continued to be pleasing and accepting. Deep inside her lurked a darkly jealous and vindictive part.

One evening she had a bitterly destructive row with her brother, which left her so emotionally decimated that she sought help. When she closed her eyes and relaxed, she drifted back to that last row with her brother. She felt the pain and hurt come up in her stomach and realized how angry and unforgiving she felt towards him and the entire family. When her inner parents came into her scene, they said some extremely cutting and unhelpful things to her. The full impact of what she had been doing to herself hit her. How unhelpful she was being to her own growth!

In her inner scenario she took those negative parents up white steps to Source and humbly asked for help. She experienced them being invited in through a pure white door and a Being of Love embraced them. A flow of love and wisdom filled them. Those parents, now wise and loving, returned down the steps to meet the hurting, jealous, vindictive part of herself. They embraced and all judgement and criticism dissolved. She glowed with the warmth of acceptance. Held in this space she no longer felt hurt or anger. She felt only forgiveness for her family.

In her imagination she spoke to her family, openly acknowledging her feelings of hurt and anger. She found that when she openly acknowledged these shadow feelings, her family accepted her. They even encouraged her and admired the work she was doing. She realized how much she had been on the defensive about her work. With this awareness Claire became more accepting of herself and more open and loving with her family. She talked to them genuinely about her feelings and was delighted when they acknowledged her work and even admitted that they admired what she was doing.

When our negative inner parents find wisdom then we can accept our shadow aspects. And when we light up our shadow it dissolves and other people accept us too. Without shadows our whole world is brighter.

Accepting our vulnerability

Many of us try to hide our weak vulnerable part behind a strong macho or independent façade. Our parents may have been emotionally, if not physically, absent and if we felt that no one was there for us as a child, we may have forced ourselves to appear very capable of looking after ourselves.

Bernadette was a strong-minded, capable, independent and tough career woman. She was brittle and slightly critical towards men. Men considered her to be aloof and tended to avoid her. When she met Jack, however, she fell heavily. Jack was a kind, caring man who simply ignored her façade and looked after the vulnerable little girl inside her. All her defences came tumbling down because for the first time she felt safe.

The adult who is very strong and independent often has a hidden part which is needy and wants to be looked after.

People often say that their parents never acknowledged their worth. What they usually mean is that they came into this incarnation with a belief in their own lack of worth. Not only did their parents reflect this back to them but if their parents did acknowledge them, they did not register it. Most of us have this belief to some extent and our task is to recognize who we are. Our mission is to recognize our God selves.

A client said to me, 'A change came over me when I realized that I don't have to have acknowledgement from other people. God always acknowledges me.' It often surprises me how many people who do wonderful work are concealing terrible feelings of worthlessness.

Robert was a gentle, outwardly confident man who was head of a large charity. He was much in demand as a public speaker and was a very spiritual and sensitive man. Yet he set up constant power struggles with his family because he was always trying to prove himself. His entire family held the same belief in their worthlessness and they all reincarnated together to work on it.

One of the ways I helped Robert to reclaim his sense of worth was by taking him back to look at many many lives of wisdom he had lived. As lifetime after lifetime unfolded and was revealed to him, he began to recognize just how much he had achieved in terms of spiritual growth.

Then I asked him to close his eyes and visualize his aura. The aura is an energy field which surrounds our physical body. Our thoughts and emotions have vibrations and the colour, smell, taste and feel of these subtle energies form the aura. If someone is sending out negative emotions he will transmit dark or murky colours. If a person has kind, loving and wise thoughts, he will radiate beautiful colours and perfume. When we live in peace and harmony we are centred in a glow of light. The more spiritual and loving our thoughts, the clearer and brighter the aura surrounding us. 'If you could see your aura round yourself what colours would you see?' I asked.

Robert immediately reeled off a list of colours and commented on how bright and rich the colours were. In his slight trance state he was totally unselfconscious. As I pointed out that he had listed the whole range of colours, he became aware of just what an incredible spiritual being he was. By now he could sense himself standing there in a huge multi-coloured aura. It gave him a really good feeling and I suggested he do this several times a day.

He then looked to see what colours his family had in their auras and realized that they too in their way were special and unique. However they were all different. When he recognized that they were all worthwhile in their own way, he could honour each of them without feeling that this in any way lessened his worth.

To recognize and honour another's qualities and gifts does not diminish the uniqueness of who we are.

CHAPTER 6

Repeating and Releasing Patterns

Our unconscious behaviour patterns can rule our lives. They keep us stuck in unhappy situations and attracting the same type of inappropriate relationships. They are like banana skins. We keep slipping on them until we realize they are there and tread differently.

When we have our eyes closed we can't see our patterns to alter them. As we open our eyes and learn to discern an inappropriate behaviour, we can make a conscious adult decision to act in a new way. The reward of mature interaction is a comfortable, empowered feeling which encourages the release of old behaviour patterns and creation of new satisfactory habits.

Facing and breaking patterns

Some patterns are quite alarming. Jeannie had been living alone for some time when she met Percy. She decided to rent out her house and move in with him because his house was bigger. After two years the relationship broke down and Percy moved out. Jeannie sold her home and stayed in the bigger house, taking on Percy's large mortgage. Percy married someone else soon after.

A few months later Jeannie met Hank. She felt her mistake first time round was fear of commitment. So this time she sold her house and moved with Hank to a much bigger one where they shared the mortgage. After two years the relationship broke down and Hank moved out. Jeannie stayed in the house and took over Hank's share of the mortgage.

Some months later Jeannie met Ray. Together they moved to an even larger house. This time she took on the whole of the mortgage and Ray paid the household bills. Two years later, when the relationship broke down, Ray moved out. Jeannie stayed in the house and now had to pay all the household bills as well as the mortgage. Ray married someone else soon after.

Jeannie withdrew from relationships after that for some time. Then she fell in love with a man who wanted her to put her capital into a business with him. I winced when I heard this and wondered if history was going to repeat itself. Luckily Jeannie had done a great deal of work on herself and was well aware of her pattern. She thought long and carefully about it all and decided not to move in with him or go into a business with him. This time she changed the pattern of her life.

At any time we have a choice to say No and break our pattern. Jeannie was not ready to until that moment. Two years later the reward came when she met and married a very different kind of man.

When we consciously break a pattern and face the pain, the Universe rewards us.

49

Creating healthy relationships

Sheila believed as a little girl that she was unworthy and bad. She wore thick glasses and had straight mousey hair. She told me that she was sandwiched between a pretty sister and a handsome brother and always thought she was ugly. Her mother was wishy washy and ineffective. Her father was strict and rigidly religious.

The child could find only one way of expressing her anger and at the same time controlling her parents. By eating slowly or refusing to eat she signalled her inability to accept love because she felt unlovable. The negative attention this attracted was better than no attention at all and reinforced her bad feelings about herself.

Mealtimes became a power struggle between herself and her father. Inevitably meals ended with her being spanked or sent to her room. Eventually she was sent to boarding school. Her parents told her it was because she was very clever and it was for her highest good but the child of ten interpreted it as rejection.

By the time she was a teenager she believed she was bad, ugly and deserved to be punished by men. She craved affection which she believed she didn't deserve, so she punished herself by starving and bingeing. She punished men by withdrawing affection.

With her belief in unworthiness she married young for security. Her belief in self-abuse and punishment ensured that she attracted a violent, punitive husband. In return she punished him by having clandestine affairs. Eventually he found out. Unconsciously she made sure that he did, for what is the use of punishing someone if they do not know they are being punished?

Her second husband was a quiet, insecure man. His first wife had affairs and he brought up as his own the child of one of her liaisons. He and Sheila had dangerously interlocking patterns. True to pattern she started an affair soon after their marriage. He, who had been so gentle, started to criticize and hit her. It was only as she told me all this that she realized just how she was responsible for causing this.

We are one hundred percent responsible for what we create. We attract people who have the possibility of behaving in certain ways.

However complex our patterns we can, with patience, unravel our beliefs and enjoy straightforward, loving lives. Sheila wanted to make a start so I asked her to close her eyes and go back into her childhood. For the first time she realized how frightened her father had been that she would die when she would not eat.

From there she slipped into another life where her father had been her brother. She had starved to death and there was nothing he could do to save her. At some deep, unconscious level she blamed him for letting her starve and was punishing him by putting defensive walls up against him and refusing to eat. At some equally unconscious level he felt guilty that he could not save her in that life. If we feel guilty others will pick this up and punish us. Because of his guilt, he was so desperate to get through to her that he beat her walls. Literally he hit her.

When she saw the frightened, desperate boy inside the father who hit her she felt an unexpected compassion and her rage towards him dissolved. She recognized that she had turned all the men in her life into her father and now she started to change towards them. She was no longer projecting her anger and blame onto them.

She became aware that her belief that she was unworthy, bad and ugly attracted men who put her down.

Feeling she was powerless to get her needs met caused her to control and manipulate rather than to state what she wanted. Naturally she could only attract a weak man who believed he was powerless to get a woman's love.

Her belief in guilt meant that she punished herself. At the same time she in turn punished men and let them punish her.

She believed her father had betrayed her in a past life and she would not trust, so she constantly betrayed men. She married a man who believed in betrayal. He married women who had affairs. As she became aware of her beliefs and attitudes Sheila started to change.

All these years the critical father voice in her head had been telling her she was a failure, didn't look nice, her hair was ugly and no one liked her. She asked him to leave. She pictured a strong, supportive, protective inner father, who stood no nonsense and told her to respond firmly to put downs. He told her to look in the mirror and reminded her of her good points. At the same time she asked the wishy washy, weak, emotional, helpless mother to leave. She invited in a new mother energy which constantly suggested loving ways she could care for herself. Sheila took many months before she could see herself differently but she did it. She created a healthy relationship with herself. Then her relationship with food and with men became stable.

We all have the capacity to become wise and loving and beautiful. It is within us all the time. We just need to remember who we really are.

Simeon and Sarah were friends to whom I felt very close. Simeon was a strong man with broad shoulders and a pleasant, open face. I knew him as a patient, kind and caring man. He was a very wise and evolved soul. His partner Sarah was slight, but powerful, also loving and caring, and very clear about her spiritual path.

Over time I observed them becoming closer as their soul link and love for each other deepened. Both had been working diligently on their own personal growth and were very self-aware. Then there was a hiccup. We found ourselves sitting round my fire one winter evening, deep in conversation about one of their problematic patterns.

For all her spiritual growth Sarah would still occasionally devastate people with a sudden streak of white hot rage. Each time this happened Simeon would remind her of a time early in their relationship when she had struck out at him verbally, humiliating him in front of others. To make it worse when he had then tried to talk to her in an effort to appease and understand, she had continued to reject him. For days he had been a supplicant. It was clearly still an issue for him. As Simeon told the story yet again, tears poured down Sarah's cheeks. 'Am I never to be forgiven. There's nothing I can ever do to put that one incident right,' she sobbed.

She looked and sounded like a little girl so I asked her how old she felt. She cried that she felt seven years old and memory after childhood memory tumbled out about what had happened at that age. When her mother was overtired, her pent up frustrations would surface until she felt out of control. She so feared that she would harm the children if she stayed that she would go out and leave them. It may only have been for a few hours but Sarah as a child did not know that. She feared her mother would never come back.

The sight of Sarah sobbing piteously, clearly seven years

old, and pleading with her mother to stay, was so heartrending that I was jolted when I glanced at Simeon. Normally so gentle, caring, understanding and loving, he was sitting quite impassively staring at the crying girl, a slight frown of irritation on his brow. There was no trace of compassion, just a stern, unbending coldness. It was as if he had a two-foot-thick wall of ice around him.

I guided Sarah to open her heart centre and heal her hurting inner child so that she could feel safe and adult. At this level she recognized that when her emotional world was threatened, she would verbally attack whoever threatened it. She promised to give her inner child the security her mother could never give her. When she was composed, loving and fully adult again, I asked her to look at Simeon, sitting so cold, rigid and tense on the sofa. 'How old do you think he is?' I asked. 'Two years old,' Sarah replied unerringly. It was exactly where I had placed him. He agreed that that was how old he felt.

When we went through a process to break down the barriers of ice so that he could connect with the feelings buried inside him, he became a hysterical child, frantically begging his mother not to leave him. His mother used to be totally unpredictable and would beat him unmercifully without provocation. She would often threaten to leave while he and his younger siblings would hang onto her ankles and beg her not to go. Whenever this happened his mother would become unbending, cold, completely without feeling and he could not get through her wall of ice.

But this time as Simeon regressed to being the terrified pleading, sobbing child, I was able to intervene as the wise mother and give him what he never had in childhood − reassurance, love and safety. No one ever heard his desperate pleas when he was a child, so how could he hear the pleas of Sarah's inner child? We cannot give what we have never received.

When she was angry, Sarah's mother could not hear little Sarah's supplication. So Sarah could not respond to Simeon's supplications when she was angry. This time, because of the wise mother's intervention, when Simeon returned to full adult consciousness, he was able to hear Sarah's cries for help. They were able to hug and talk and be close again. They had started to dissolve a negative pattern which had stopped them from getting really intimate. However entrenched our tricky patterns have become, with willingness and commitment, we can change them.

Peace, harmony, tranquillity and serenity are choices for everyone.

CHAPTER 7

From Denial to Honesty

One of the commonest defences we have is denial. An ostrich buries its head in the sand and pretends there is no danger. We too protect ourselves by ignoring feelings and by denying what we really know.

Denial, however, is a form of self betrayal. Our body will draw it to our attention with aches and pains or lethargy. As we take the risk of acknowledging our hidden feelings to ourself, we place our foot on the ladder to wholesome relationships and vibrant health. The next step is to acknowledge our true feelings within our relationships. However painful the truth is, it is better than the rumbling thunder clouds of deception and dishonesty for honesty has a resonance which lightens and heals. Only when feelings are claimed and aired can an intimate and joyful relationship develop.

At some level we know everything.

'Forgetting' the truth

All her life Angie had been a born organizer – petite, attractive and seemingly as hard as nails. If she was involved in a business it was inevitably a success. Then her husband was promoted, so they moved to a new town. He was busy setting up his new job and worked all hours. Her children had left home and she felt alone, unsupported and lost. Uncharacteristically she became depressed and despondent and sat at home all day crying. She went to see a clairvoyant who told her to be careful as her husband was deceiving her, that divorce was a possibility and she would move to a new house within the year.

Angie told me crossly that the woman was a charlatan and had told her a total load of rubbish. 'My husband would never look at another woman,' she told me. 'He's always worshipped the ground I walk on. As for any possibility of divorce, that's so ridiculous, it's laughable.' And she added defiantly, 'There's no way I'm moving again now I'm just beginning to settle here.'

They moved house quite unexpectedly within the year, which surprised her. Her husband seemed to work all hours at his new job for about two years and then things gradually began to improve. Angie was getting her life together in their new location and had decided to start another business with a neighbour when her husband told her that he realized that she was unhappy and she could have a divorce if she liked as he had been having an affair for a couple of years. He said it had been over for about six months. Angie said afterwards. 'I never realized how powerful denial was. The moment he told me about the affair I knew exactly who the woman was and when it started. He didn't have to tell me anything. I knew it all. It was as clear as daylight. But I never thought about it until that moment. I suppose I just couldn't cope with it before.'

Denial is a coping strategy which does not ultimately serve our purpose on Earth. We are here to become transparent conscious Beings.

When Angie and her husband brought everything out in the open and talked it all through, she felt so much better. She was able to acknowledge that she was often rigidly controlling and at other times needy and demanding and could see how this had undermined their relationship. He was able to acknowledge his anger and guilt. Their relationship became closer than it had ever been. For the first time ever she felt contented.

The value of emptiness

Susannah was married to Denis. She described him as a nice but boring guy. He was gently ineffectual and could not meet her needs. However he was consistently safe and solid. The bubbly Susannah often felt trapped and irritated. To admit to these feelings would mean she would have to examine the basis of their marriage. So she denied the feelings and created diversions instead. There is nothing like a little chaos for getting the adrenaline going. Her diversions gave her a sense of excitement and aliveness. From time to time she would fall in love. Her unconscious made sure she chose someone safely married or rejecting of women so that it never developed into a dangerous affair, but the excitement of being in love was a tonic.

Even the misery when it all fizzled out was better than boredom.

Sometimes she overspent, which worried Denis, so the agony of doing the accounts and feeling bad kept her mind off the underlying emptiness. Mostly it was enough to throw herself into organizing a dinner party or bridge evening.

One time, after she had fallen particularly inappropriately into infatuation, she talked it over with me. She began to see her pattern of creating excitement to deny the emptiness within her marriage. 'The bottom line is that I've either got to change my attitude to my husband or leave the marriage, isn't it?' she said thoughtfully. She was silent for a while. 'Then I suppose you'll say that the emptiness in my marriage reflects the emptiness within me?' she went on. 'Well I do feel empty. Kind of disconnected a lot of the time, especially the last few years.'

The awarenesses she came to that afternoon shook her. She realized that she looked for safety and stability outside herself, from Denis. When she felt insecure she leant on him. When she felt stable, the emptiness set in and she tried to fill it with external excitement. So she saw that she swung between feeling insecure or feeling empty, with stable periods in the middle.

Susannah decided to shelve any decisions on her marriage for several months. She knew that if she did not heal herself she would only attract in another dependency relationship. She worked on her inner child and talked on a more consistent basis with her inner wise parents. The most important thing that she did was to go back to daily meditation. Like most of us she found it hard to still her mind but Susannah had a streak of determination and whether she had a good meditation or not, she sat for twenty minutes each morning in the same place in the house and focused as well as she could on calm, quiet breathing.

We all have a calm, quiet pool in our centre where we can connect with all the help we need. When we still the outer chatter of our minds sufficiently we can connect with this place. Here we can find all the answers, all the strength, all the confidence we need.

While Susannah was rushing around and denying her emptiness, the space could never be filled. Now that she had acknowledged it and decided to meditate, she found a new connection with her Higher Energies. Through meditation, she started to raise her consciousness and to connect with gifts and potential which had until that moment remained latent and untapped. She started to find a core of contentment inside herself. She discovered that she was very intuitive. She joined a healing circle and started to write a book she had always wanted to write. Within a few months, because she was no longer yoyoing round her husband, he began to blossom. She realized she had been taking all his psychic energy with the pulling and pushing she had been doing.

As long as our problems are denied we cannot do anything about them. When we bring them to conscious awareness we can start a process of change.

Denying our needs

Lorna was a solid lady, sensibly dressed with invariably neat hair. She was a pillar of her church, was on the committee for two local charities and served on the Parent

Teacher Association of her children's school. She was respected by all.

She came to me because of her insatiable urge to nibble sweet things. She felt out of control. In Lorna's life everything she said or did was aimed at earning the respect of others. She looked after everyone else and denied her own emotional needs. She fed her need for sweetness with sugar. All through childhood she felt unwanted, so she tried to become the perfect child. The only way to do that was to be her sister Penny, her mother's favourite who could do no wrong. 'It's funny,' Lorna said. 'They even used to call me Penny at school. The teachers and the other children and my Dad too, were always getting my name wrong. I couldn't have made that happen, could I?'

As she remembered how she had longed to be like Penny and even used to doodle her sister's name instead of her own, she realized how she had thought herself into being Penny. By doodling Penny's name, she had impressed her subconscious mind that she was called Penny. Naturally she radiated this out so people picked it up and reflected it back to her. They called her Penny and, yes, she made it happen.

We are totally responsible for everything that happens. We make other people behave as they do towards us by the energy we send out.

She totally denied herself and her own needs. At the end of the first session she casually mentioned that she had had cancer but it had all been cut out and dealt with! Cancer is a classic symptom of denial.

Lorna let go of her need to compensate with sweets very slowly. But gradually the perfect façade began to crack and she got in touch with the frightened, messy, unhappy inner part of herself which she had tried to deny for so long. When she experienced that this part of her was lovable too, she softened. Then she could let love in and cut sweets out.

Our true motives

At some level we know everything so we are in denial when we say, 'I didn't mean to.' When we tell someone we didn't mean to hurt them, we are not being honest. Of course some part of us meant to hurt them or we would not have done it! 'I didn't intend to bump your car,' means: I bumped into your car because at some level I intended to do so but it was not conscious. 'I forgot to pick up your clothes from the cleaners,' means the part of me that chose not to pick up your clothes was stronger than the part that wanted to pick them up.

Once we say to ourselves, 'This happened. Therefore unconsciously I intended it to happen so what was going on for me?' we can start to look at our deeper motivations. If the result of our actions is that the other person is angry we are usually doing something to express our anger passively so that we do not have to take responsibility for it.

The one thing that was guaranteed to make Sonia furious was the car or house being left unlocked. It made her feel insecure and unsafe. When she first met Greg, he looked after her and always locked up. As their relationship progressed he often 'forgot' to lock the doors. Sonia used to rage that he could not be relied on. She did not trust him to look after her.

When I spent a few hours with them one afternoon it was perfectly clear that she emasculated him. There was always the faintest hint of disapproval from her about everything he did. On the surface he adored her but underneath he was furious. He could not express it directly for fear of losing her, so he pushed the anger down into the unconscious and 'forgot' to do the things that Sonia liked.

Acknowledging needs

In many co-dependent relationships couples exist for twenty, thirty or forty years of marriage in this gloomy world of dishonest denial. Many of us are very good at denying our own needs. Inside many a big strong independent person is a tiny little child screaming, 'I want to be looked after.' The big strong person will usually deny this little voice until there is a crisis. If we deny our needs how can we expect other people to see them? If we deny our needs how can we expect to see other people's needs?

Gill told me that she spent her entire marriage being cheerful and busy. Her husband was often away on business. Her children grew up and left the nest. No one gave her a second thought as she quietly fell to pieces under her cheerful façade. She said, 'They never see my need so they don't know I need them.'

She had a housekeeper, an excessively bustling cheery woman, who came to look after the house whenever she went out for a day or even several days. The housekeeper talked incessantly when she arrived home, so Gill would delay her return so that she did not have to speak to her. Gill suddenly realized that her housekeeper had not spoken to anyone all day and that she had never seen the woman's need. 'How could I see her need,' she reflected, 'When I was so busy denying my own?'

There are many bright cheerful people who deny the depressed part of themselves. These people are often tired because it takes a lot of energy to keep an aspect of ourselves in denial. Life presents us with mirrors. If we put up a cheery façade and deny our depression, we will attract depressed people into our immediate environment, in exact proportion to the extent of our denial.

Hilary was pretty and bubbly with a bright smile and sad eyes. She resented and disliked her work situation and used up a lot of her available energy in covering up her depression.

On the last occasion she came to me for a session she said, 'I'm feeling great but a few weeks ago I had to force myself out of bed. I said to myself, "You will get up. You will go to work. You will do a good job. Don't you dare lie there," and I got to work every day.'

As I reflected this back to her she became aware that a very depressed little girl was lying in bed, with her authoritarian father ordering her about. No wonder she was depressed! Under depression there is always anger and she felt angry and powerless against her negative father. What she really needed was reassurance and help from a strong, supportive, encouraging father who would not let anyone undermine her. When she realized this she closed her eyes and asked her negative father, that internalized voice that kept ordering her about, to leave her inner scene.

Then she imagined her strong wise father coming in to talk to her and encourage her. With his support she faced all the people and situations at work. In her inner scene she imagined herself calmly but firmly reclaiming her power. She saw everyone responding to her with respect, with admiration and in a friendly way. As she experienced this her anger evaporated and she felt good. She felt her energy return and her depression lifted.

Hilary started a daily programme of listening to her wise father. With his support she dared to speak up for herself. She stood no nonsense. She felt more confident. Within two months she had taken a decision to leave that job whatever the consequences. I saw her at a party and she had relaxed and become softer. Her smile was genuine so that it touched her eyes and dissolved the sadness. She felt comfortable to be with.

Depression indicates a need to take a decision. When every decision presents us with a difficulty we tend to stay stuck and that embeds us more and more firmly into helplessness and hopelessness. When we deny and cover up our underlying feelings, there is nothing we can do to change our state until time, fate or death brings change to us. When we look within and take a decision the Universe will support and help us.

Decisions decide our destiny and give us the power of inner peace.

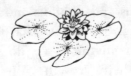

CHAPTER 8

Reinterpreting Life

I remember receiving a letter when I was particularly out of sorts. I read all sorts of rejections, criticisms and put downs into it. A few days later when I was feeling sunny and happy I picked it up and reread it. I could not imagine how I perceived my original interpretation!

Our Personality Self imputes difficulties, problems, lower interpretations and dubious motives to the actions of others. Our Higher Self knows that we are in service to each other and that anything we do to another will at some level serve their growth. We would not do it otherwise for our Higher Selves are always in perfect accord.

Remembering this, it is appropriate to examine the actions of others and intuit what their higher motive could be. Then we can review, re-interpret and joyously reintegrate our past.

The love behind abandonment

In some areas our negative mind sets are so strong that we continue to interpret life through distorted lenses whatever happens.

Tanya was adopted when she was six weeks old. She could hardly bear to talk about her natural mother who gave her away. She interpreted her adoption as a total rejection by her mother. Of course, she saw her father's abandonment of her mother as rejection too. All her relationships were sabotaged by her belief in rejection. She expected rejection. She set up rejection and she made rejection her reality.

Finally, pushed by her disastrous relationships, she came to see me. She was small, thin, almost fragile, and looked ready to run away.

I found Tanya difficult to work with. She found it very hard to open her heart and seemed determined to stay stuck in her hurt feelings. However we persevered and at last, after several sessions, she had what was for her a mind blowing revelation. *She realized that her natural mother so loved her that she gave her away for her highest good.*

Tanya's heart centre started to open. At her next session she moved to a much higher level of awareness. She met her Higher Self and learnt that the lesson she most needed for this life was to let go of personal attachments. Out of a great soul-level love for her, Tanya's mother had volunteered to give birth to her out of wedlock and let her be adopted at great personal anguish, because this is what Tanya's soul most needed in this lifetime. In doing this her mother had gone through terrible torment, rejection by her family and heartache.

That session really threw Tanya. The façade of her great defences started to crack. She had to start to let go of feeling hurt, rejected and blaming and take responsibility for her life.

The love behind money

Something similar happened to Gerda. She too believed that her mother did not love her. Her parents were only interested in money and in material things, or so she told me. 'My mother never held me or told me she loved me. All she ever said was how much I cost her to keep,' Gerda complained. The corners of her mouth turned down. I could see that she had made this complaint many many times in the past. 'The last straw,' Gerda told me, 'was when my father died. I wrote to mother after the funeral and told her how unloved I felt. All I wanted was to know she loved me. She wrote back an itemized list of how much I had cost her through my life. I haven't written since.'

She was angry, hurt, bewildered and upset. I listened to her for some time, then I asked her to consider that perhaps her mother equated love with money. 'And perhaps,' I suggested, 'when she wrote to tell you how much she had spent on you through your life it was her way of saying, "I loved you so much I spent all this money on you. I loved you *this* much."'

Gerda sat stunned. Suddenly she said. 'You're right. She's saying she loved me *that* much. They did spend everything they could on me. I remember how they worked to get together the money for my gym lessons – and they couldn't afford my skiing trip but I so much wanted to go that they got the money to send me.' And the floodgates of memory opened.

The next time I spoke to her she said she had written to her mother. She told her mother that she realized now for the first time just how much she must have loved her to spend all that money on her . . . and how much she appreciated it. She had a letter back from her mother. It was the first letter Gerda had ever received from her that was tender, warm and loving in tone. It did not mention money. Gerda laughed as she read it to me. 'All this time she's been trying to tell me in her way how much she loves me but I never understood it.' It was the first time I saw Gerda look radiant. She had discovered that by reinterpreting our lives, we find joy.

Pre-life agreements

Almost invariably, when we are abandoned in childhood it is a pre-life agreement between us and our chosen parents. We have made that decision at a higher level to serve our growth.

Mike's mother ran off with another man when he was two. His father could not cope with him and his brothers, so he was put into care while his brothers went to relatives. On the surface Mike was a charming affable man with an eye for the ladies. Underneath he held a deep, violent mistrust and rage towards all women. His heart centre was full of pain.

During a channelling session he learnt that before he was born his mother had offered to give him this experience of abandonment, which he needed for his highest growth, out of her great soul love for him. She had arranged that when Mike was two she would meet a great love from a past life. Their attraction would be so irresistible that she would run away with this man, despite the fact that she loved Mike and his brothers so much.

After this channelling, Mike's attitude began to soften and change. He began to see things differently. He had put a missing piece of the jigsaw of his life into place. *Every time we put in a piece of jigsaw we have a new perspective on the whole and we get nearer to inner peace.*

I do not condone abandoning children. I do know, however, that at a spiritual level there is often a very different reason from the perceived selfish one.

Whatever Mike's mother's highest intentions she will, at a personality level, because of her thoughts of grief, anger and confusion, have accumulated karmic debt because of her actions. These debts she willingly took on board in this life in order to offer Mike the lesson he most needed to learn. He learnt that only fear separates us. *Love can never be abandoned.*

Moving on

Karen claimed that her relationship was totally wrong. It was difficult, boring and not serving her in any way. I explained that she was in the perfect relationship for her to learn whatever she needed to learn or she would not be there. She was most certainly there because it served her to be there.

We are always where we are NOW because we have placed ourselves there to learn. At any given moment we are in the perfect place with the perfect people for our growth.

As we recognize this we can say to ourselves, 'I placed

myself in this position for a reason. What is it?' The sooner we understand, the more quickly we can move into a different space.

From the perfection of NOW she could more easily see how the relationship served her. She admitted it kept her safe. It kept her blaming her husband instead of taking responsibility for her life. It kept her feeling bad and that was a familiar place for her to be. When she had admitted these things to herself, she was able to consider the possibilities open to her. The relationship continued to serve her for about a year before she left.

We are always in the perfect situation or relationship at this moment NOW. It may not be right for us this afternoon or tomorrow but if we are in it NOW it is the right one for us NOW. It embodies the perfect lessons we are choosing to learn at this moment. So we are called on to learn the lessons and then we can move on.

David felt a total failure. Both his marriages had ended in divorce and now his current relationship was in difficulties. He thought he must be a terrible person if he could not sustain a relationship.

We looked at what happened in his childhood and at his life patterns. He began to see that he had learnt a great deal from both his marriages and that the second one was completely different from the first. His current relationship too was quite different. He was behaving in a more mature way and making choices he would not have been capable of making in his two marriages.

He reinterpreted his perceived failure as success. He realized that he had succeeded in learning what he needed to in this relationship and it now served his Higher Purpose to move on.

A failing relationship may well indicate that we are

stuck in certain patterns, causing conflict. But it can often be an indication that we have learnt all we need to in that situation and the karma has ended, so it is time to leave.

David let go of guilt and belief in failure and started to feel at peace with himself. In the past, unless a partner died, we had the opportunity to learn about only one relationship because society demanded that marriage was for life.

Now, however, in this New Age, everything has speeded up because of the changes ahead. As mentioned previously, most of us want to learn our lessons now so that we can move up faster in Earth school and be ready for the coming changes. We may, therefore, have several relationships or marriages in one lifetime in order to grow more quickly, without going through the process of death and rebirth.

We are therefore called on to let go and move on when a relationship has served its purpose. It serves no one to stay in a 'completed' relationship. It is like expecting a schoolchild to stay for years in one grade when he is ready to study the next one.

Criticisms belong to the critic

James was smarting under a sense of injusice. His father had said to him, 'You'll never do anything with your life.' James said to me in fury. 'I've got a good honours degree, I've been promoted every year in my job, how dare he say that to me.' I reminded him that people only ever talk to themselves. *When someone says something to us which seems hurtful, inappropriate, even untrue, it helps to remember that they are talking to an aspect of themselves.* James became thoughtful. He said 'It's true. Dad has never fulfilled his potential and he knows it.' By reinterpreting his father's comment, he began to feel compassion for his father instead of resentment and rage towards him. *Genuine compassion is oneness, which is a state of inner peace.*

When I was ten I was invited to be a bridesmaid to a cousin on my father's side whom I had never met. I was thrilled and excited. My mother and I went to Wales for the wedding. I had a beautiful long lilac coloured dress with a rich velvet purple sash, a flowered headdress and a matching posy of flowers.

Waiting to go to the church I felt a million dollars, like some beautiful princess. I floated along in a dream. My mother turned to me and said, 'You can tell they'd never met you. Usually they only ask pretty girls to be bridesmaids.' I wanted to die! I walked up the aisle wishing the floor would swallow me up. I spent the day trying to be invisible.

When I learnt that people only talk to themselves, I could recognize it was my mother's problem and let it go. My daughter healed this more completely for me some years later when I was telling her this story. She burst out quite spontaneously, 'Oh Mum. You were such a pretty little girl.' Yes. I could choose to hear that and feel O.K. about that incident.

It is never too late to heal distressing childhood feelings.

Josie was constantly complaining about her husband. She blamed him for her limitations. A friend asked her to go on holiday with her. 'I can't go because he'd say I was selfish to spend his money on galavanting around having a good time.' 'Has he ever said anything like that?' I asked. Josie paused. 'Er . . . well . . . No.' She thought again and frowned. 'Actually he always tells me to go off and do things.'

She flushed as she came to the awareness that it was the voice in her own head that told her she was selfish to spend her husband's money on galavanting around. She was projecting that voice onto her husband. She realized suddenly that she was afraid of going away without him safely beside her. She also became aware that she was the one who was afraid of spending money. From that it was a small step to recognizing that she did not believe she deserved to have a good time.

Josie placed herself constantly in lose/lose positions. If she went on holiday with her friend she felt bad and guilty. If she did not go, she felt angry with her husband. 'Imagine you really deserve to have a wonderful holiday and your husband wants you to go,' I suggested. 'What would happen then?'

She closed her eyes and experienced new feelings and emotions. 'I am having a really good time and coming back relaxed and full of interesting stories to share. My husband is pleased to have the space on his own. He's glad I'm happy and we are closer than we have ever been before.'

'And what if you felt really deserving and still made a decision not to go away?' I asked.

She closed her eyes and connected with her feelings.

'That's O.K. too. I'm planning a holiday for myself and my husband instead,' she replied, looking quite relaxed about it.

'So either way you win?'

'Yes. Either way I win. That feels really good.'

When we hear unloving things from others, when we feel ourselves to be unlovable, then we need to go back and see again and hear again with new eyes and ears. It is up to us to reinterpret it and place ourselves in win/win positions.

Winning perspectives mean inner peace.

CHAPTER 9

The Soul's Journey

The journey of a soul is similar to that of a human being. It will progress from being a baby, through all the developmental stages until it is an adult. Even then experiences will change a person, mature him and allow him to grow in wisdom. There are gifted children and wonderful young adults, yet we do not expect them to have the maturity and experience of an old person. It is the same with souls. There are horrid or beautiful souls in all stages of development. Our growth comes in learning to accept them. To do this it helps to understand how we evolve.

When a baby is newly born it is completely helpless. It cannot survive on its own and will die without attention and love. We automatically respond by giving it the protection, care and love it needs. Because it is so young we do not expect anything of it but enjoy it for what it is, knowing that if we cherish it, it will happily develop its potential.

New souls in their first incarnation are the same.

Spiritually they are developing the base chakra, which is the survival centre. They are learning about survival in a human body on Planet Earth, so they often choose to live in primitive, undeveloped places far from the complexities of civilization. Learning to survive is so tough that they often choose very short lives in different survival situations. There are, of course, many wise souls who incarnate amongst them. Very new souls are not incarnating on this planet at this time. It is as if the whole tribe of man has chosen to move on to a new place and it no longer provides a suitable environment for new young ones.

After a number of incarnations, a newish soul may come out of the 'nursery' and choose to experience an advanced society where there is more to learn and where there is one baby soul to several mature ones. Because it still cannot look after itself it will need an environment where it is cared for by others, so it may choose to be born disabled or mentally handicapped or into a simple rural community. Of course, many evolved souls also make those choices to repay karma, speed their growth or to help others. At one time baby souls were often born into Down's syndrome bodies but now these opportunities are frequently being taken by old souls offering teaching to those around them.

Every human being is born into the right place at the right time for their growth. As a world we need to be aware of the needs of countries with high baby-soul populations and give them the succour and help they require to develop. A group of baby souls who incarnate together simply will not be able to improve their conditions or move and adapt from difficult situations. It is no use talking to them like adult souls. They need to be cherished and helped.

Learning independence

As a baby grows into a toddler and pre-school child it becomes more independent. Because it is learning about security, it needs very structured boundaries to feel safe. During the 'terrible twos' a child often has tantrums in an effort to assert who it is and test these boundaries. As it develops to school age this calms down as a new world of learning opens.

The soul who has passed through the first set of lives to the toddler stage is developing its sacral chakra, the centre of emotional, sexual, security needs. It only feels safe if it is bounded by organized religion, disciplined society or a tight family set up.

These young child souls are the proponents of dogma and the upholders of strict moral values in a family. Security is more important than freedom or self-expression. They feel safer in dictatorships, however uncomfortable. If their family or community structure falls apart they are emotionally torn to pieces. They are powerless to fight for their rights. An angry toddler may hit its mother or younger sibling but it will not attack anyone bigger and stronger. So the toddler group of souls are capable of persecuting the weak, starting internal wars, doing horrendous things to protect their religious dogmas or secure community way of life. They repress free-thinking spirits. This soul age group can ostracize others from the community or family for getting pregnant or divorced, having an affair or upsetting the equilibrium.

If a young child really cannot get what it wants it will become apathetic as it endures hopeless conditions. In some countries there are apathetic masses of toddler souls being exploited and seemingly unable to move out of their conditions. They need help from the family of man as would any frightened toddler.

Learning about power

When the child becomes a teenager it is full of ideas and energy but is often confused. It wants to put the world to rights, to help the underdog, to explore and to proclaim its freedom to be an adult. In so doing it may rebel against convention. It may need the support of other teenagers, all trying to prove their identity. If its energies are not directed it may move in an aimless gang of like-minded youngsters who cause trouble and violence. It needs to dance, explore and express who it is. The teenage soul group are learning about freeing their personal power.

In this soul age group are the fun loving, jet-setting people often with no seeming respect for convention. Where groups of teenage souls incarnate together without any outlet for their energy, there is violence and unrest. They will not be subjugated like a young child. They will rebel and fight. If their energy and capabilities are channelled wisely they can accomplish great feats. So, after a few lives of disturbance, kicking over the traces, rebellion and pleasure seeking, the young adult emerges.

Learning about success

The young adult soul is keen, ambitious and intent on success and power. This soul group is symbolized by the young men with drive and enthusiasm who are determined to be millionaires before they are twenty-five. With that as their goal they are unstoppable. They are striving, materialistic and do not mind treading on others to get where they want. These young souls are often materially successful, money is very important to them. Where young adult souls head companies, profits are more impor- tant than ethics. Decisions are taken for the personal advancement of self before the good of the whole. Where they head countries, riches and image are vital. They create disturbance and wars but their energy, properly guided, can make the apparently impossible happen.

Groups of this soul age tend to build up lots of karmic debt. They make money by exploiting others. In their quest for personal power, they crush the free will of others.

Learning about maturity

A country of mature souls will be challenged when groups of very young souls incarnate amongst them and they feel either worn down or invigorated. Teenage energies tend to be disruptive. Parents of teenagers breathe a sigh of relief when their young reach adulthood. A country with a fair percentage of teenage souls is unlikely to be too peaceful. A country with all teenage souls is inevitably unsettled. Repression would cause rebellion. Mature, imagi- native guidance is needed to calm the unrest and harness the potential and energy.

The toddler and young child, the teenager and young adult souls are the ones who are earning lots of karma, sometimes building up huge burdens of debt by careless cruelty, lust, fighting, subjugation of others and misuse of power.

Learning about service

When younger souls develop into mature and old souls, they want to repay the debts incurred in earlier lives. This is why older souls often appear to have very difficult lives.

When we grow into maturity, happiness, commonsense, equality and justice seem more important than money and power. Mature souls are less materialistic and more reasonable. They are opening their heart centres so they see everyone's point of view and want everyone to have a fair share. Where they incarnate amongst new baby souls, toddlers or young children souls, they help to guide and nurture these younger souls very caringly.

As we become older in life we become wiser, non-judgmental and more introspective. We have less energy and may be world weary. We spend more time looking for the meaning of life. And old souls are less likely to choose to be born rich or spend their lives seeking money. They have done all that so they tend to be non-materialistic. Money and personal power have lost their magnetism. Because they know of its lack of importance, they tend to devalue it and often have financial problems.

An old soul will have great insight, awareness, sensitivity, intuition and wisdom. They are opening up to the spiritual energy of the third eye centre. They need time for inner work for their values are more spiritual. Conventional morals based on control rather than spiritual awareness mean nothing to them. They will be working for the good of all mankind, concerned about the Planet and are on a spiritual seek-and-search. A young soul may be drawn to spiritual development work out of curiosity but will not have the dedication to stick to it as an old soul will. Old souls know of the divine essence of all things and respect the sanctity of life. They will not willingly hurt anyone or anything.

Where old souls incarnate and are heard and valued, peace and a rich quality of life reigns for they attune to the highest good for everyone. Just as a child can regress to babyhood when there are problems or a middle-aged or old person can act abominably when threatened, so we can all regress to the behaviour of a younger soul age *in extremis*! While a younger soul will aim for his materialistic pathway by his twenties, the mature and old soul, who is sensing something more important in life, may not find his path until he is much older.

Older souls tend to have an inner knowing about past lives. It is not surprising. If we take a baby or young child to the seaside every week, it forgets. An older person paying a visit to the seaside will retain a memory of it. A young soul having several visits to the Earth will forget but an older soul will have at least a faint recollection of what it was like. The precognitive flashes and the understanding will be there.

In order to help the transition taking place on Earth right now, more old souls are being born. No longer in spiritual retreats, old souls are in the communities with wisdom, understanding and wider perspectives to help the human family. There is great hope for the future.

In this New Age, our planet is moving into the constellation of Aquarius which is introducing a much higher energy to the planet so that people can live with unconditional love and mastery over their lives. Many old souls here now are preparing the way for those illuminated souls who will incarnate soon to bring these new energies to Earth. We will move from a third dimensional planet, where we live in physical reality with karma, to a fifth dimensional one where we live spiritually with grace.

I believe that as we understand more why people and countries behave in certain ways – acting inevitably from their soul level – then we can give appropriate help. Also, we can feel more comfortable about happenings initiated by a young soul which are seemingly incomprehensible if we are expecting the behaviour of a mature soul. Everything at the spiritual level is perfect.

Choosing our name

Most people accept that the incoming soul chooses his time and place of birth. The position of the planets at the time of our birth have a psychic effect on us and their great energy will continue to exert an influence on us, challenging, supporting or moving us forward at different times in our life. The moment and date of our birth is very important and carefully chosen before we decide to incarnate. This is why astrology is a spiritual science.

The baby is in the mother's womb for nine months. Throughout that time nourishment passes from mother to baby. Emotions and telepathic messages pass in both directions and the baby impresses on the mother the name it wishes to be known by. Every letter has a corresponding number and each number has a vibration. So the name that the child is given on birth contains all the vibrations of his mission in this life. So as our name is spoken our lessons resonate within us. Our name calls us and reminds us of why we are here.

Each vowel resonates in a different chakra. If we use an abbreviated name, we are perhaps only working on part of our lesson at that time. This happens for many children. If we change our name or choose a new one, we will still have our original lessons but will also be expanding to other ones. In general terms, women do this more than men by acquiring a new surname on marriage.

According to numerology, which is the spiritual science of numbers, every letter of our name has a number and each number corresponds in the cosmos with our lessons. There are nine *life paths* which indicate our main chosen mission so, as a new soul coming in, we start on the first life path. There are different ways of *expressing life* through our work or vocation, from 0 to 9, so the new soul will start on number 0 and progress through to 9. Our *soul urge* is our inner motivation. Again the numbers we follow run from 0 to 9. So we progress on a grid chart to cover all the combinations of life path, life expression and soul urge. As we learn our lessons at each vibration we get a tick. Sometimes we have to do an aspect of a life several times. Each time it gets more difficult until we earn pass marks. Then we move on to the vibration of the next number.

Numerology

LIFE PATH

To find our Life Path, we take our date of birth and write it out in full. Take the day, the month and the year separately. Add the numbers together and reduce to a single digit if necessary. Then add the resultant 3 single numbers together, and again if necessary reduce to a single digit. For example:

Mahatma Gandhi was born on
2nd October 1869

$$02/10/1869$$

DAY	02	reduce to single digit	$0 + 2 = 2$
MONTH	10	,,	$1 + 0 = 1$
YEAR	1869	,,	$1 + 8 + 6 + 9$ $= 24$ $= 2 + 4 = 6$

To find the Life Path simply add together the 3 resultant single numbers

$$2 + 1 + 6 = 9$$

This shows that his Life Path is governed by a 9.

Steven Spielberg was born on
18th December 1947

$$13/12/1947$$

DAY	18	reduce to single digit	$1 + 8 = 9$
MONTH	12	,,	$1 + 2 = 3$
YEAR	1947	,,	$1 + 9 + 4 + 7$ $= 21$ $= 2 + 1 = 3$

To find the Life Path simply add together the 3 resultant single numbers

$$9 + 3 + 3 = 15 = 1 + 5 = 6$$

This shows that his Life Path is governed by a 6.

General Challenges of the Life Path Numbers

1. To learn the benefits of independence, self-confidence and leadership.

2. To learn how to serve, support and be diplomatic.

3. To learn how to bring joy and wisdom through communication.

4. To learn to be stable, dependable, organized and practical.

5. To learn flexibility of outlook and the constructive use of freedom.

6. To learn how to give and receive love wisely and create harmony.

7. To seek an understanding of life and spread it with wisdom.

8. To learn how to harmonize the spiritual and material.

9. To learn to be compassionate, selfless and release unproductive situations.

LIFE EXPRESSION

Our Life Expression shows the way we express our talents and abilities, so it indicates our vocation.

To find our Life Expression we take our full name at birth. Using the chart below allocate a number to each of the letters in your name. Add up the numbers in each name separately, and if necessary reduce to a single digit. Then add the resultant single numbers together, and again if necessary reduce.

1	2	3	4	5	6	7	8	9
A	B	C	D	E	F	G	H	I
J	K	L	M	N	O	P	Q	R
S	T	U	V	W	X	Y	Z	

for example:

Martin Luther King, born as Michael Luther King

M I C H A E L
4 + 9 + 3 + 8 + 1 + 5 + 3 = 33 = 3 + 3 = **6**

L U T H E R
3 + 3 + 2 + 8 + 5 + 9 = 30 = 3 + 0 = **3**

K I N G
2 + 9 + 5 + 7 = 23 = 2 + 3 = **5**

6 + 3 + 5 = **14** = 1 + 4 = **5**

So his Life Expression is governed by a 5.

General Characteristics of the Life Expression Numbers

1. Original, ambitious, full of drive and energy.

2. Tactful, sensitive and cooperative.

3. Joyful, optimistic, sociable.

4. Dedicated, reliable, a sense of application.

5. Dynamic, communicative, adventurous and artistic.

6. Responsible, generous, determined and home-loving.

7. Analytical, self-sufficient and questioning.

8. Business-like, organized, intuitive and achievement-orientated.

9. Generous, sensitive, broad-minded and humanitarian.

SOUL URGE

Our Soul Urge shows our heart's desires.

To find our Soul Urge we add the numbers of the vowels of our full name. Using the chart allocate a number to each of the vowels in your name. Add up the numbers in each name separately, and if necessary reduce to a single digit. Then add the resultant single numbers together, and again if necessary reduce. For example:

Paul McCartney,
born as James Paul McCartney

J A M E S
  1 + 5   = 6

P A U L
  1 + 3   = 4

M c C A R T N E Y
    1   1   5 + 7 = 13 = 1 + 3
                              = 4

$$6 + 4 + 4 = 14 = 1 + 4 = 5$$

So his Soul Urge is governed by a 5.
(NB In numerology a 'y' is treated as a vowel.)

General Desires of the Soul Urge Numbers

1. To be independent and lead.

2. To be the power behind the throne.

3. To be creative and expressive.

4. To have security and structure.

5. To have freedom, excitement and adventure.

6. To be surrounded by love, beauty and loyalty.

7. To have space and time to delve and investigate.

8. To be successful and wealthy.

9. To be philosophical and understand the Universe.

In school, if a student fails one of his subjects but passes in the others, he may be allowed to go up to the next grade and redo the failed subject at the same time as he does the work of the higher grade. Life's lessons are just the same. If we fail at a karmic lesson but move on anyway, the vibration of that number will move on with us and we will have to face those challenges as well as our new ones in the next incarnation. When we have successfully completed the numbers and passed all possible Earth tests we do not have to incarnate again. When we reach this level we may choose to incarnate to help others and will choose numbers where we can resonate with those we wish to teach.

We face ourself with our own challenges. Everyone eventually has to do them all. The more quickly we do the things that feel difficult, the speedier our journey to the highest vibrations. There is no chance, chaos or confusion. We are all very much part of an ordered Universe. We all flow to the rhythm of Love.

Resonating to the rhythm of love brings inner peace.

CHAPTER 10

The Seven Levels
of Life

At school our work is designed to expand our understanding each year, so the information we learn in Class One forms the groundwork of our learnings in Class Two. When we reach the upper echelons of school we are expected to remember the early lessons. However it is easy to forget or have missed a few important lessons.

As spiritual beings our experiences are organized so that we open up through the seven spiritual levels (chakras) of survival, security, power, love, communication, vision and oneness. However, we may have forgotten or missed a few vital learnings on the way. It may be that our soul generally is working at level four but we are dealing with money from level one and sexuality from level three. Those are the areas of our life we need to address. We can see which spiritual level we are working from at any time by looking at our attitude towards whatever we are doing.

The chakras and our needs

When we are trying to meet our basic survival needs we are operating from our base chakra, the densest of the spiritual energy centres of the body. If we need a place to live, cannot get a job or feel abandoned we will be in fight or flight mode. This means we are on red alert to fight for our existence or flee from danger. When our survival is at stake, our base chakra opens wide and releases to us the information we need to secure our basic human needs. It also picks up from loving, safe, secure Mother Earth reassuring and helpful nurturing energy.

Once our survival needs are being met we can operate from higher chakras. The sacral chakra is orange and deals with our sensual and security needs. When we aim to satisfy our sexual or emotional desires we are working from this centre. The urges of our lower three centres are survival, security and need, so if our energy is in our solar plexus we are compelled to do that which helps us feel more powerful or makes us look good in the eyes of others. Here we need to boost our self-image.

At the higher levels our motives are altruistic. At the heart level we act out of caring and compassion. At the throat level we are serving the highest good of the planet. At the third eye we are selfless instruments of the Divine.

The chakras at work

Our spiritual level will govern our attitude to our job or business. If we are operating from our base centre we work primarily to survive. Our compulsion will be to get food and shelter for ourselves and our families.

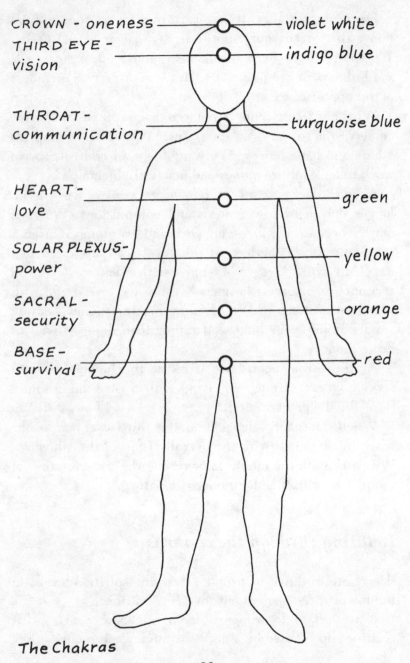

CROWN - oneness ——————— violet white

THIRD EYE - vision ——————— indigo blue

THROAT - communication ——————— turquoise blue

HEART - love ——————— green

SOLAR PLEXUS - power ——————— yellow

SACRAL - security ——————— orange

BASE - survival ——————— red

The Chakras

From our sacral centre we earn money in order to have things that gratify our emotional, sensual or sexual needs. We want money for a big house, good food, a smart car and holidays or we desire it to draw in attractive members of the opposite sex.

Working for a living from our solar plexus we drive ourselves in order to gain status. We need to impress others and have power. We want to be in control, so we work to amass more money and material objects.

As our energy rises to our heart centre we are no longer driven by lower needs and compulsions. We earn money because we love our work and are doing it from a genuine sense of service. At this level we cook or garden or clean with love. We study with pleasure. We do accounts or manage a business because we love it and with a high ethical sense. We are now making money because we are doing something well rather than doing it well to make money.

At the throat centre we work at the higher levels of service where earning our living will involve doing something for the greater good.

When our energy level is in the third eye we do our work in alignment with the overall vision of the Universe. We work with the intention of raising the consciousness of the planet or in total harmony with nature.

Relating through the chakras

We relate to different people at varying spiritual levels. In the lower three centres our love is conditional.

If we relate to someone from our base centre, that relationship is based on a need for money and security. Sex at this level is prostitution. We may be selling our body for money in order to pay the rent. In a relationship, the unspoken deal is that we will be available for sex in exchange for financial security.

In our sacral centre we have relationships to meet our sexual or emotional needs. Commonly we nurture our partner in order that we get emotional strokes in return.

When we relate from our solar plexus we are co-dependent or needy. We stay in relationships because we fear we will fall apart if we leave. We would rather stay in a bad relationship than face the horror of being alone.

Once we reach our heart centre we offer unconditional love to friends and partners. There are no strings attached to our relationships. We relate with delight and harmony and are with people because we want to be, not because we feel we have to be.

Relationships from the throat centre are based on total trust and honest communication and a genuine desire to do our best for everyone.

When we relate from our third eye we choose friends and partners who serve with us for the Highest Good.

The chakras and our garden

I knew an old man who filled every part of his garden with vegetables and rusty old things that might come in useful some day. He worked in his garden with the sole aim of growing vegetables, because he was terrified that he would not have enough money to live. He begrudged even a bite of leaf to a snail. He thought flowers or a pond were a waste of space. He was operating from his base centre for survival and certainly did not trust the Universe to meet his needs.

Eileen created a very attractive garden when her children first went to school. She devoted a lot of time to it. It looked immaculate but the children were not allowed to play in it in case they damaged the plants. When we love something but we cannot share it, we are attached to it and in our sacral centre.

The person who has a superb garden to offset his beautiful house and to impress others is in his solar plexus. He gardens for effect rather than enjoyment.

At our heart centre we garden because we love it. We delight in working with nature. We feel for the plants. We create a garden for others to enjoy.

The person who is operating from his throat centre will create a garden to serve the planet in some way. I was talking to a young man who was building a permaculture garden in order to work with nature and create food for his community. He was planting a forest garden with nut and fruit trees. There were no fruit cages to stop birds. Instead there were bird tables to encourage them! He told me there was enough for the birds and for them. He smiled as he watched the squirrels chasing up and down the branches. 'They have 20 percent of the nuts and we have 80 percent,' he told me. Everything in his garden was done for the highest good of the planet and the creatures in it.

At the level of the third eye we create a garden to serve God.

The chakras and our home

When we buy a house we do so from a variety of emotions or needs. At the lowest level we buy a house because it gives us financial security or to make money in boom times. We may buy it because filling it with nice furnishings will satisfy our emotional needs. Or we may purchase it with a view to impressing others.

At the higher levels we buy a house because we love it and also to make a warm, loving nest for others. We create a home for the overall good of the family or to serve others in some way.

At the highest level any house we bought, however small, would be dedicated as a Light Centre.

The chakras and having a baby

It is sometimes helpful to check out our motivation for having a baby. There are many people desperate for babies, who have them for lower reasons.

At the base centre level we will have a baby because we hope it will look after us in old age. Some girls and women have babies because they will get housed by their local Council. In some countries women have babies because they get more money begging with a child.

Many of us have a child because we need someone to belong to us and meet our emotional needs. If a baby satisfies this longing, we are bringing in a soul from the level of our sacral centre.

If we have a child in order to look good in the eyes of the world, to continue the family name, to give us a sense of power over someone weaker then ourselves then we are in our solar plexus. Then we have a child to boost our lack of confidence in ourself.

At the heart centre we love babies and want to give a child a home. It is not important whether the baby is our blood or not.

At the throat centre we know all are one and we offer ourself in service to the incoming soul.

At the third eye we call in a chosen soul and parent it for the highest good of the child.

The chakras and creativity

We write books, compose music or paint with different energy levels, which will shine through our creation.

When we create in order to make money to survive we have no high intention. We work solely for commercial gain because we need to.

If we are in our sacral centre, our creations will be emotional, sexual, sensual or erotic and we will be doing it to make money to buy things which satisfy our desires.

In our solar plexus, we write books, paint or compose to court admiration. We may write to gain influence over others but our primary motivation is financial gain.

When we create from our heart centre, we do so because we love to write, we love music and painting and enjoy expressing ourselves in this way. We do it because we want to, not to make money. Because of this money flows to us!

At the throat centre, we create because we are spreading a message via our chosen medium for the upliftment of others.

At the third-eye level we are channelling. Consciously or unconsciously we are in touch with the Divine levels, allowing ourselves to bring forth aesthetic, beautiful or inspirational works. We are spreading a vision.

The chakras and self-protection

We all try to protect our spiritual centres if we feel threatened and one way to do so is by putting on fat.

If we feel vulnerable about our survival, we physically protect our base centre with fat. We need to store for the future because we don't trust the process of life, or we may hold onto old emotional patterns because the familiar feels safe. Then we put fat on our buttocks or thighs. I talked to a woman who told me she had always had big thighs until she did a past life regression, during which she went back to the source of the energy block.

She regressed to a life as a healer, when she had been burnt at the stake as a witch. In the session she was able to release all the fear she had been holding and over the next few weeks the weight literally fell from her thighs. I did not know her before the regression but I can vouch that she had very slim hips when I met her some time later. She was also an excellent healer. Military men march on their heels to prepare their base centres for action. When they stand at ease they hold their hands over their base centre, front or back, to protect it.

When we need to protect our emotions or our sexuality we cross our legs or put fat on our abdomen over our sacral centre.

The classic beer gut belly protects the solar plexus and

indicates an underlying lack of self-esteem or personal confidence.

Sometimes we physically protect our heart centres by becoming round shouldered. Or we can armour our heart centre by building a great big muscular chest.

Thyroid problems would indicate a vulnerability at the throat centre. We are even more likely to protect it by getting a croaky, hoarse voice or even losing our voice so that we don't have to express anything dangerous.

We protect our third eye by frowning or wearing our hair over our face. A headache would indicate that something is amiss here.

As we become aware of the spiritual levels we are operating from, we can make conscious choices to let go of the lower and choose something higher.

Our life is our mission. Make it a peace mission.

CHAPTER 11

Coping with Loss

Spiritually aware people know that when someone dies their spirit walks through the door to the next part of their soul's journey. An increasing number of people reporting near-death experiences are bringing back confirmation of this from their personal experience. These are people who have clinically died but return to life again. They universally report that when they saw their dead body they turned away from it towards a Light or a tunnel with Light at the end of it. The Light was so infinitely loving that they wanted to go into it but someone in spirit told them it was not their time and they must return to their body. They invariably describe a reluctance to return to physical incarnation and a complete loss of fear of death.

So at a spiritual level our personal grief at someone's death is selfishness. We mourn solely for our own loss. Our grief is our attachment to having them with us in a physical body.

However, human beings have emotional needs and responses. Every thought we send to someone is an energy impulse. Eventually these thoughts form psychic cords which attach to the other person. The more passionate our feelings, the stronger the cord. Jealousy, anger, need, lust and hurt are very passionate feelings. Unconditional love does not form a cord. It leaves others free. The strength of these cords dictates how we mourn our loss. Mourning takes as long as it takes us to uncord from the other person. The average time it takes for cords to dissolve naturally is two years, although it can take much longer.

Blocked grief

If we sublimate our feelings and deny our human emotions we will have to deal with the blocked emotions later in this life or another, for anything suppressed clogs our chakras. Denial of grief solidifies liquid emotions into crystals or ice which will eventually cause damage in the physical body.

Janey was widowed twice within a short space of time. It was all too much to bear and she simply disassociated from the feelings. At her second husband's funeral, she was the life and soul of the party. She felt nothing because she was not emotionally there. She remained like that for three years, slightly spaced out and out of touch with her emotions. This meant that the cords between her and her second husband never dissolved properly. She could not commence the mourning process until three years after his death, by which time her supportive network had disappeared and she nearly collapsed under the backlog of emotions.

Our attitude to the death will depend on our mental set, our beliefs about our lovability, our ability to cope alone, and our thoughts about life and death.

Grief about loss is cumulative if not expressed. Occasionally someone 'puts a brave face' on the death of a parent, a close friend or a husband and everyone thinks they have no feelings or that they are very stoical. Then, when a distant relative or the cat dies, they fall to pieces. It is simply that the backlog of grief has caught up with them.

Our emotional responses will depend on how much permission we give ourselves to cry, be angry, hurt or fearful at our loss. And in the years after the bereavement our physical state will depend on this emotional response.

Sudden loss

If a loved one is ill before they die we have an opportunity to accept their impending departure and to loosen the cords which bind us. This helps them to pass more easily and also assists our mourning process. But if a loved one dies suddenly, the cords between us are torn out and we suffer from shock, grief and neediness. The severed cords will reach out from our chakras like antennae trying to link into the person who is no longer there.

Mandy adored her father. He was a kind, solid man who coped with everything. All her life he had been there for her. He was like a rock through all her tantrums and tears. She could talk to him about all her fears. Indeed he was a pillar of strength for everyone and it was too much for him. One day he collapsed and died.

Mandy fell into shock and acute grief, alternating with rage at her father for abandoning her. Now that he was gone she dumped her anger inappropriately on other people and was disconcerted and hurt when they retaliated.

At a spiritual level she was very aware that he had been freed from human bondage and she should be rejoicing with him at his release from the physical body. But at an emotional level she felt like a child, angry, hurting, needy, demanding.

Her emotional chakra was split wide open by the sudden loss. The severed cord was searching for her father's energy. Where this happens the bereaved person usually puts that cord into someone else's chakra for emotional support.

Mandy tried to put this cord into her husband's sacral chakra to compensate. He knew that this would have caused an emotionally dependent relationship, so he steadfastly refused to accept it. As a result, the mourning period was very traumatic. Because she had been dependent on her father's energy, its sudden withdrawal was rather like quick withdrawal from drug dependency.

So she had to find herself very quickly and emerged a much stronger and more independent woman.

Guilt and negative feelings

Jack had a very different relationship with his father, yet he too fell to pieces totally after his father died. All his life he thought he hated his Dad for being domineering and demanding. He expected to feel only relief that the overbearing old man had gone. To his horror he found that the old man's voice followed him everywhere, criticizing him and reminding him he could not manage alone.

He found himself thinking about all his guilty secrets and feeling vulnerable and exposed. He felt the old man was watching him, judging him. Jack believed he was a bad son and deserved to be punished. Even deeper down he held a belief he could not manage without his father and had built a large tenacious cord into his father's solar plexus, which is why he felt so lost when his father died.

He needed to talk about his guilty secrets so that he could see them non-judgmentally accepted. The best way I know of releasing guilt is to share the secret with a non-judgmental person we trust, who hears, understands, empathizes and still accepts us, whatever we have done.

Sure enough, Jack started to feel a release of tension as he shared the actions from the darker side of his life. I then gently pulled out the remainder of the cord from his solar plexus and helped heal this chakra so that his confidence began to return. He was very sensitive, and looked greatly relieved when I told him that his father had not passed over properly and was influencing him from spirit. He had wondered if this was happening because he could feel his father around him and these were the times when he felt worst, so he was glad to have his suspicions verified. He was able to close his eyes and see his father in front of him. He asked the old man to go now and leave him free to get on with his life. His father left for the Light with little reluctance.

Jack was able to cry then for the first time genuine tears of loss for his father. It was a turning point. He was able to resume normal life and even started to remember happy times with him. He never felt his menacing presence again.

When we miss the death

Often people are upset if they are not with a loved one when they die. Gregory felt relieved when I explained that the force of his attachment to his mother had been holding on to her. She did not have the energy to detach from her body and pass over while he was there. So, although she loved him, she had had to wait until he left the room before she could gather enough strength to leave her body and die.

Similarly Maggie was hurt and upset when her mother died before she reached her bedside. 'Why didn't she wait until I got there?' she cried.

I asked her to close her eyes and make a connection with her mother. Her mother appeared very vividly in front of her. She told Maggie that it had been her time to go. 'I knew that your great need of me would have held me back and prevented me from passing, so I left before you came, but I loved you very much.' So the fact that she passed before her daughter arrived did not mean that she rejected her or did not love her. In fact she told Maggie that she would stay with her and help her from the other side.

Dealing with anger

Joseph's father died in an accident. The night before he died he appeared to Joseph in a dream and said 'Goodbye'. Then he walked away from him across a river towards a beautiful Light, turning only once to wave. Next morning the police called with the news of his death. Joseph had great difficulty accepting his death because there were so many unresolved issues between them. In the course of time and therapy he began to realize how much his father must have loved him in order to come to say goodbye in this way. When he recognized the love, Joseph was able to give himself permission to explore his anger towards his father.

When we believe we are not loved it is too dangerous to explore tricky feelings for fear that the little we have may be destroyed.

It is when we feel loved that we feel safe to express our frustrations, hurts, fears and angers. And then these feelings too can dissolve and no longer run our lives.

It was not until he had ventilated his anger that Joseph could really grieve.

Anger blocks the grieving process for it holds the cords in place so they cannot loosen and detach naturally.

Communicating with the spirit

Sometimes it is not we who hang on. There are times when the departed spirit does not fully leave the planet and hangs on to the Earth life through someone who is emotionally linked to them. We all know of ghosts who haunt people and places. They are sad or angry spirits and need our compassion and prayers.

Frieda's mother died ten years before she came to see me. From the other side the mother had hung onto and controlled her daughter. The daughter's fear of her mother was such that the cords remained intact despite death and she was manipulated strongly from the other side.

A simple cord cutting as described in my first book

Light Up Your Life was not enough to separate the two of them. Their karmic connection was very strong as was the mother's unwillingness to leave her daughter. We worked together for several months before she could be freed. A case as extreme as this is very unusual.

The mourning process for very aware souls who are prepared for the passing can be very different.

A friend of mine, whose wife died of cancer, remained in constant touch with her spirit for some weeks after she died. It was as if she had never left him.

He visited me three weeks after her death and when he sat by me and gave me her crystal to hold, her voice was as loud and clear in my ear as if she had been physically talking to me. From spirit she had no jealousy and constantly encouraged him to meet other women, expressing the hope he would settle down again because that was what he needed. She continued to look after him and talk to him, only gradually moving further and further away as he began to cope better.

Jim, on the other hand, was less evolved. So was his wife. He went through agonies of guilt after she died about all that he had left undone in his marriage. When he met another woman whom he wanted to marry, his guilt and his wife's anger holding him from the other side, was set to doom this new relationship.

I asked him to relax to a deep level where we connect easily with spirit, then to close his eyes and visualize his wife in front of him, so that he could express what he had not been able to say then. Her spirit entered the room and stood angrily beside him. He felt her angry presence and for a moment became too fearful to work, until I reminded him that love always dissolves anger and that her anger was only her fear.

Jim became stronger and opened his heart. He expressed all his regret and sorrow about what he had left undone. At that her anger palpably softened. He heard her say, 'I forgive you' and she left never to haunt him again.

In my early days as a therapist I had a client, Madge, whose partner murdered his first wife. The man was a well-educated, mild, unassertive person. His wife constantly flaunted her affairs and publicly humiliated him and the children in many ways. She also had a wild, uncontrolled temper and would hit him and the children.

One day the worm turned and he hit her back. She fell, knocked her head and died. In panic he hid her body. When she disappeared, everyone assumed that she had carried out her often repeated threat to leave him.

Several years later when he was living with Madge, his wife's body was found and he was imprisoned for murder.

Madge came to see me for therapy. Her partner was not a sensitive but she was. She told me that from the moment she had moved in, the dead woman was in their house, implacably angry and vengeful. The moment Madge spoke of her, the dead woman's spirit came into my office and refused to leave for several hours. This happened on each visit. One day I was sitting with a friend on a tube train telling her about my dilemma. Suddenly my friend leapt up with a shriek. Talking about her had brought the spirit of the dead woman to us. She had sat, ice-cold and malevolent, next to my friend.

That decided me to do what I should have done before. I called in a medium to talk to the dead woman. She persuaded the wife to let go of her hatred and desire for vengeance and go to the Light. The dead woman's mother had passed over many years before and was waiting for her. As she saw her, she turned and went towards her, leaving at last.

I was told that because of her husband's action, the woman's life had been cut short by nine years. She would have the opportunity to reincarnate for those nine years, possibly as her current husband's child, in another incarnation.

A friend of mine, a wise and beautiful evolved soul, died in an accident in her twenties. She and her boyfriend had been very much in love. After she died he could sense her loving presence but was not psychic enough to see her or talk to her.

Through a mediumistic friend, the girl came back and told him that she loved him but had had to leave. She said that she had detached herself from him so that he was free to have another loving relationship. He very quickly met someone else and my friend appeared once more to their mutual friend to send her blessings to the new union.

Passing over is not always easy, especially if we are attached to our earthly life.

Brian was very spiritual and clairvoyant as was his mother. His father, however, was of lesser understanding. When he told me that his father had died, I asked if he had had a good passing. 'Well, no actually. Dad took three days to pass. He didn't want to leave his material possessions and what he knew.' He was haunting all the psychic members of the family and making a thorough nuisance of himself. So Brian had had a tricky few days constantly talking to his father until he finally persuaded him he was dead and that it was time to move on.

Patty had an abortion. She lit a candle and said a prayer for the departing child but it was not enough. The child kept coming to me in dreams, presumably because I was the link between her and Patty. In the dreams she was always out in the cold alone.

She needed the energy of prayer and love to help her on her way. Then she was able to go. Never assume that someone has passed safely, though of course most people do. Just as our grief can hang onto a loved one and keep them earthbound, our prayers, hymns and loving thoughts can help them on their way to the Light.

When we send prayers and love to those who are passing over, whether we know them or not, it helps them to find peace. And when we create peace in others we find it within ourselves.

Mac's father had been getting frail and for months his spirit had been locked in his body. It was a long-drawn-out ending. Mac was sitting by his bed at the moment when his father died. He saw his spirit rise up and leave his body. Then his father danced an ecstatic and lively highland fling over his discarded physical shell. It was a wonderful celebratory dance of freedom. He then turned and left for the Light.

When someone we love dies we may care to remember that what is death to the caterpillar is life to the butterfly.

CHAPTER 12

Empowerment

Some people are total victims. They think the world owes them a living or they blame everyone and everything except themselves for the state of their lives. Their frightened eyes plead for help as they send out subliminal cries for someone to rescue them. Most of us have a little bit of victim in us, the part of us that would like a magic wand to make everything better. Victims are furiously angry with themselves and the world. As soon as someone tries to help them, they resist all efforts and eventually turn on the rescuer. Victims are abusers.

The pattern changes for victims the moment they realize they are responsible for their lives and that they have the power to change things. Then they can decide what they do want and picture it clearly and vividly, which sets their unconscious mind in a positive direction. Affirmations help to increase their confidence and willpower. Creating a wise parent puts them in touch with their own inner wisdom, which helps them decide what steps they can take. This starts the journey to empowerment because the wisdom, the decisions and the steps have come from inside them. We all have the power within.

112

The rage of the powerless victim

Bruce phoned me in a very low mood. Having left the police, he now found himself as a bodyguard for two prostitutes who needed protection. They were key witnesses in a slander case involving a well-known figure and one was under a death threat.

For some weeks a national newspaper had paid to keep these two girls in the height of luxury. They were bored out of their minds. Maria, blonde and slim, was 20. Her friend, Andrea, dark and vivacious, was a few months younger. They spent most of the day in a drugged haze, freaked out by pot, alcohol and thirty cigarettes a day. They became locked in an emotional lesbian partnership.

In their boredom they would order Bruce around, slam doors in his face and treat him like dirt. Bruce felt frustrated and very angry.

Then the newspaper decided to cut costs and installed the girls in a small house in the middle of nowhere. Having lived on the proceeds of prostitution they had become used to high living, nice furniture and bright lights. They felt imprisoned by the tiny house, but they were terrified of going out.

They sank more deeply into dope. Maria would have wild, uncontrolled outbursts of rage. More than once Bruce had to take knives away from them as they were about to attack one another. The guards started to lock away anything that could be used as a dangerous weapon. They were so afraid that Maria and Andrea would kill one another that they took it in shifts to sleep outside their bedroom doors.

When the girls weren't having screaming tantrums, one or other would withdraw into a deep sulk. Maria particularly was depressed, felt claustrophobic in the small rooms and cried a lot. She was paranoid about security in the house, imagining anyone coming to the door was going to attack them.

This was the atmosphere in that strange household when Bruce phoned me to see if I could help. Both he and his wife had been clients of mine and I liked them very much. However when he described the scenario to me I quailed. He said he had talked to Maria about taking responsibility for her life and although she was angry and blamed the whole world for her predicament, she had said she wanted help.

I gulped and said that if she would ring me herself to make an appointment I would be prepared to talk to her! 'I must be mad,' I thought to myself as I put the phone down. I really assumed that she wouldn't phone. But phone she did and ten days later her appointment was due.

When the car drew up outside my house I went out to greet the slim blonde who got out. *All I could see coming down the drive towards me was pure white light.*

At that moment I was seeing the Divine within Maria and I knew she was a very special person. I clung tenaciously to the vision of white light through rage, hurt and hostility directed at me over the next months and years. Many was the time I almost gave up. However we both held the vision and the true Maria gradually emerged.

Her story was truly horrific. Her mother was inadequate. She constantly felt hopeless and powerless and Maria was the fifth of seven children, all of whom had different fathers. Her mother later told her that her real father had raped her when she was a small child and her sister told her that he had raped her too. Maria never knew who or what to believe.

Her mother married her step-father and the two of them constantly argued and fought. Her mother was violent towards the little girl and often urged her step-father to hit her too.

The frightened child's greatest moments of hope were when her mother would wake her in the night and say they were leaving home. The two of them would creep out of the house and walk the streets for hours. 'I used to hope and hope we could get away but there was nowhere to go and so we always went home,' the girl told me, her eyes still filled with anguish at the memories.

Maria was only nine when one of her brothers started to rape her consistently. When she told her mother, the woman who should have been her protector didn't want to know. Maria was pregnant when she was twelve. She did not dare to tell anyone so she was five months pregnant when it became obvious and she had an abortion. Then she was taken into care.

Her childhood was a story of betrayal by social workers and sexual abuse by a variety of different men. Because she felt so bad about herself, she started sleeping with boys when she was fourteen. At least she thought they'd like her then, but all that happened was she felt worse and worse about herself.

At the age of twelve, because she kept running away from the children's home, she was put into a high-security institution with eighteen-year-olds, mostly drug addicts and women of the streets, where they treated her like a hardened criminal. By the time she was sixteen it was a small step to prostitution.

At that first appointment, Maria felt desperately angry and helpless. She was terrified of life. After she had told me some of what had happened to her, I explained that we do not live in a chance Universe and that we do choose our parents and our childhood circumstances in order to learn from them. I also told her that we have within us the power to change it all and that our thoughts can transform our lives. She realized that all the time she was angry with the abusers, she was giving them power over her life.

I explained about the vision of white light I had seen walking down the drive! To my delight she accepted it all. As an old soul the Universal Truths resonated and the scales fell from her eyes. She left radiant with smiles.

When she went home she went cold turkey on the drugs and Bruce told me that she was a different person.

Of course, for someone so damaged, there was a long way to go. Although she was twenty in chronological age, she was like a child emotionally. One minute she would be sad, lost and crying, another she'd become sulky or red with anger and moments later her eyes would cloud with terrible fear and the pain of her memories. But more and more often her wonderful smile would peep out and her face would be alive. It was some time before I grew to know her joyous, pure laughter, so infectious that she could lift anyone's spirits in a moment.

She went for a spiritual reading with a medium I trust and was told that her core was pure white light and that she was a very old soul and a healer. She assured her that she would find a good relationship and have much happiness. That buoyed her up for a while.

I now know that Maria has many faces. I often see her as earnest and eager to learn, full of wonder at all life can offer. I hear her wisdom as she rocks a serious group with the simplicity of her observations. I rejoice in her lightness as she opens up to her true spiritual potential.

Whenever I think of Maria, I feel humbled. She came

into this life as a pure white light into a very muddy background. Inevitably some of the mud stuck and affected her personality self. However, she has consistently worked to understand and forgive all who abused her. She has created a loving relationship with her parents and step-father. She now attracts totally different people into her life who love and support her. It is as if what happened in the early part of her life happened in another life so much has she changed.

There are many beautiful souls locked in horrible circumstances just waiting for the Truth to rekindle their light.

When we look for the Divine Light in others we open the door to their real selves.

Waking up to our power

Many of us never find our life purpose because we are carrying so much dead wood. If we saw a rose bush that was full of dead wood we would prune it back however ruthless it seemed in the full expectation that it would blossom prolifically the following season. Yet we are so much less compassionate or firm with ourselves. Most of us hold onto old relationships and friendships long after they have served their karmic purpose. We hold onto jobs we dislike, clothes that we never wear and ornaments that no longer delight us.

When I worked with Henry he described his job as boring. He had been doing the same work for many years and wanted a change. 'My boss really gets up my nose,' he told me. 'I just dread getting out of bed in the morning and facing the day.'

He told me that his chief pleasures in life were his wife,

his children, his grandchildren and his hobby. He really would like to earn a living from his hobby and he reckoned he could do so.

After we had looked at his situation, he decided that he was 75 percent dead and 25 percent alive. He realized that if one of his rose bushes was 75 percent dead, he would take drastic action. With this awareness he took a decision that he would give up his job and make a livelihood from his hobby. He had enough spare cash to support himself and his wife for two years. He left my office looking younger, alive and joyful. What is more, he was enthusiastic about the future.

However, when he went home and told his family they were horrified at the thought of him giving up his job. They would rather the man they loved was safe but 75 percent dead than that he was alive!

When he came back to me six months later, his back was playing up and he felt unwell. We reassessed the situation and he decided that he was 80 percent dead. He was not living. He was gradually dying.

That was when he decided that, come what may, he was going to give up the work he hated and do what he wanted for a living. He was going to live for a living.

When we take decisions to live by what we love, we feel at peace. We feel enthusiastic, which means en theos, *living with God. We are alive on our Path.*

Tony was a big, burly, jovial man. He was always the life and soul of the party and radiated bonhomie. When I saw him in my office, I saw a different person.

'It's my mother,' he confessed. 'She gives me no peace. She's always on at me to visit her and when I do she does nothing but nag me. I can't do anything right and I feel really angry with her.' His face was red. His hands clenched and unclenched. He looked extremely uptight. He was not at peace. This big, burly, usually jovial man had given away his power to his little sparrow-like mother. He gave her the power to upset him.

He worked to reclaim his sense of self-worth. Then he felt at peace. Then he no longer allowed her to upset him. He was then truly powerful.

Bob told his brother Jason that he ought to visit a certain specialist about a pain he had. For the sake of peace and against his better judgement Jason let himself be influenced. He went to the specialist. It turned out that he could not help and it cost Jason money he could ill afford. He felt angry with Bob and also with himself.

Jason's anger robbed him of inner peace because he had given his power away. Jason understood that when we let ourselves be influenced, we give that person power to direct our lives. The next time his overbearing brother told him he ought to do something, Jason deliberated and then took his own decision about what to do. He had listened to his intuition. It was the right decision. It worked. He felt pleased with himself and he was empowered.

If we let anyone influence us in any way we let them rob us of our power and our inner peace. Our power is inside us.

When we walk our truth no one can influence us. We seek no external acknowledgement or validation. It comes from within. We are empowered and at peace.

CHAPTER 13

Connecting
with the Earth

The base chakra, sometimes known as the root centre, is where we ground ourselves. Just as a tree needs roots to keep it firmly secured in the ground, so our spiritual essence needs to be earthed.

Not surprisingly, the base chakra is governed by the element earth. It embodies the earthy qualities of dependability, how practical or down-to-earth we are about life, our ability to survive hardship or overcome difficulty.

Our life support

A plant needs time to adjust if it is uprooted and so do we if we are moved. During drought conditions or in infertile soil a plant sends out deeper roots to try to support itself. Those that do not become unstable or wither. The same applies to humans – if our base centre is strong we will strive to adapt to new conditions. If a plant is abused in any way – uprooted, trampled, sprayed with toxins, flooded or parched – we would expect it to need a great deal of tender loving care before it re-establishes itself.

In the same way, if we have left our partner or a loved one has died, if we cannot pay our bills or are being evicted from our home, if we have lost our job or are terrified of not having enough money or our life is in any way being threatened, we will be struggling for survival and we will need to give ourselves tender loving care in order to re-establish ourselves.

We would not expect a plant to flourish in stony ground. It needs rich, nourishing earth to give of its best. If we are living in a rich, nourishing environment we will be flowering. However if we are living in stony ground it would be sensible to take steps to enrich our lives so that we can flourish and flower to our full potential.

If our emotional support system is insecure we need to create new friendships or deepen those we have. It may help to build a reliable support network by joining clubs or societies where we feel we belong or to take up new interests. We may need to ask for help knowing that not until we feel grounded and secure can we expand and develop safely.

If we are financially insecure we may need to look at our income and expenditure and take some practical decisions. If this does not seem possible we need to change our attitude to money.

If our mind sets keep undermining us, it is time to change our belief system to one which supports our growth. The more secure and solid our foundations of self-worth are, the safer we will feel in our lives.

Reacting to stress

The base centre contains all the information we need to survive physically on the planet. When our survival feels threatened, the base chakra opens wide and releases this knowledge. This activates the adrenal glands so we are ready to react to the danger. We are on red alert.

It is absolutely fine to be on red alert occasionally, when we really do need to act to deal with physical danger. In coping with the danger we use up the adrenaline. However, when our base chakra opens to help us to deal with imagined danger or psychological threat, it equally activates the adrenal glands and sends surges of chemicals round our body with no outlet. Then we remain feeling twitchy and anxious until they are eliminated. If this happens frequently, it helps to practise relaxation techniques and especially slow rhythmic breathing into our base centre. A panic attack occurs when we perceive or imagine a danger. Our base chakra releases instructions for a massive boost of adrenaline to be released to deal with it. It is like being told there is a tiger waiting to pounce which we cannot see. It is no wonder we panic!

Nina was a young woman in her twenties, thin, anxious and droopy. She richocheted from one disastrous relationship to another. Life to her was full of threat and danger. Whenever she was exposed in a queue or in an open space she would close down and limit her world. Then she would have a full-blown panic attack.

Gradually I taught her to ground herself in those circumstances, really root her feet into the safety of Mother Earth, and then open herself up to the world around her by truly seeing and experiencing her surroundings. Her panic attacks ceased and she started to be alive instead of a shallow breathing, anxious being who was more dead than alive.

We are here to experience Earth conditions and live.

If we exist as a wilting plant with no life force we are not fully present in our incarnation.

The need to face fears

A young married woman came to see me because she had been having panic attacks for the past six months. She told me that she was happily married and that they had started apparently out of the blue.

As she began to talk about her life it emerged that she had discovered her husband's infidelity eight months ago. He refused to discuss his 'fling' and they had never talked about it. But the whole basis of their relationship was undermined. Because it was never aired, all her fears, angers and insecurities surfaced but there was no release. There was no reassurance and therefore no way to calm them down. There was no safety.

She did not know that it was reasonable to expect her husband to talk about what had happened, so she kept quiet and her terror manifested in panic attacks. We discussed her rights to know and to express herself.

She went home and faced him. She insisted that she had a right to know what had happened. She listened to his story and tried to understand. She learnt how he had been tortured by guilt. At the same time she expressed her own fears and her rage. Then he said he was sorry. As he realized how she had suffered, for the first time he truly reassured her. At last she felt safely rooted in her marriage again and the panic attacks stopped.

Hot flushes result from surges of adrenaline. When they occur during the night, our unconscious fears are activating our fight/flight mechanism. Hot flushes during menopause indicate that we have fears about our future. It is hardly surprising as it is a time of change for many women, occurring as it does when our children are leaving the nest and we are coming to terms with being no longer young. Are we facing a future without an active role as wife and mother? Are we afraid of being usurped by a younger woman? Perhaps we would like to start a new career or interest but have lost confidence? Perhaps our partner is taking early retirement? It all means change. Externally, we may appear assured and in control. If we have hot flushes it is a warning to us that we are feeling insecure about some aspect of our life.

Blushing and flushing are also adrenaline responses indicating that our base chakra is preparing us to face danger. Fear is there to remind us that we need to look at an aspect of our lives.

The physical effects of imbalance

On a physical level, our base centre governs the large intestine, the rectum, legs and feet. Imbalances here could manifest physically as haemorrhoids, prostate problems or sciatica. If we are too yin, hold on to everything and sit on our tensions, we will tend to be constipated. Then we need to relax and let go. If we are too yang, we tend to have diarrhoea, indicating a desire to rush forward without getting the most out of our experiences. Lower back pain indicates deep insecurity. When we worry about our financial situation or our material welfare it is as if the base of the stalk of the plant is being pinched.

Each chakra has a colour associated with it. The colour linked to the base centre is red, which is the slowest, heaviest vibration. Red symbolizes dynamic life force, even a thrusting aggression. It is from the base chakra that we get the energy to get moving and make a success of life, to go out and get business, to stand up for our rights. It is from here that we activate the passion to chase our vision.

Lightning flashing around in the skies is a wasted energy and potentially dangerous until it is safely conducted to earth. Unless we earth our intuition, our visions and ideas, they too remain floating about in the ether, unfulfilled and unfulfillable.

If we are not grounded, our base centre is too yin and we may live in a fantasy world. Or we may be attracted to other worldly experiences or even drugs.

Whenever we feel spaced out, distracted, not quite with it, we are slightly out of our body and unable to feel our feelings. This means we do not feel our pain but at the same time we do not experience aliveness and joy. For some of us who slip readily in and out of our bodies, it is very easy to become ungrounded. It may be that, at some level, we are escaping from life, but it can be an extremely uncomfortable experience. Fluorescent lighting in super-markets often has this effect.

If our spirit jerks out of our body we may not come back in straight. In an even more extreme, but not unusual case, if we are woken suddenly our spirit may have had to crash-land back into our body. We may be very crooked. In this case we may have a headache, feel dizzy or have a stomach ache. If we are badly out of alignment we may feel very ill with all the symptoms of twenty-four hour flu.

How to come back in line

If we are just slightly out of alignment and feel spaced out or dizzy, a few drops of the Bach flower remedy called Rescue Remedy, walking, dancing, anything fun and active should get us back to normal again. Anyone who has lectured to a group on a soporific afternoon or after a heavy lunch knows the benefit of fresh air, stretching, jumping up and down, or even a tea break.

When we are badly out of alignment we need to relax completely. Spiritual healing helps us to enter our bodies fully. Sometimes we may need to go to sleep. Then our spirit leaves our body completely and we can come back in more calmly.

George was in pain following an injury to his neck. For a week he felt dizzy and uncoordinated until he went to the osteopath and had it realigned. Then the pain lessened and the uncomfortable spaced out feeling went. The pain had kept him slightly out of his body.

In times of ancient wisdom, the priest or priestess kept an injured person out of their body and free of pain by mind power, while operations were performed and the physical healing started. Modern medicine attempts the same effect with anaesthetics, which weaken our auric field.

We all need to ground ourselves constantly. One of the best ways is to walk in nature and reconnect with the earth. We pick up earth energies through the base chakra, and subtly absorb peace and beauty, leaving us feeling safe and relaxed.

The core of Mother Earth is a safe, solid, secure energy. It is a nurturing, loving, caring place and our base chakra swivels downward like a search light to seek this security, which is always there for us. If we are living in a high-rise block of flats, our base chakra cannot pick up the subtle earth energies and can become depleted. In these circumstances it is especially important to get out into nature when we can.

Our internal generator

When our base centre is working properly, we succeed in the material world as we bring our life force to our daily experiences. We then have the energy and vitality to bring our creative ideas into operation.

The base centre is the home of our kundalini energy. This is our life force, sometimes depicted as a serpent coiled up ready to rise up the chakras to link with the God force. When it rises, it opens us up to enlightenment.

If an army is preparing for battle the soldiers must be ready for action, so they march, striking their heels on the ground and so activate the red centre. All war dances involve stamping the heels on the ground to raise the kundalini energy. It is impossible to feel half-dead, lethargic or out of our body when we are performing a war dance.

I talked to a young woman after I watched her walking. She was putting her toes down first, and I soon realized that she was tiptoeing through life itself. Her boyfriend was involved with another woman and she tiptoed round him trying to get him back, never daring to speak her feelings. She tiptoed round people in the office and they ignored or devalued her, calling her a wishy-washy intellectual.

I explained to her about the energy of the base centre and suggested that she take a walk each day, exaggerating putting her heels down first. The effects were quite startling. Within days she had found the energy to tell her discomfitted boyfriend to decide between her and the other girl. Within two months she had quit her job and found a better one where her qualities were valued. 'I'm not going to be a pushover any more,' she said. I smiled at the aptness of her expression. Of course it is not so easy to push over something with proper foundations.

Inevitably she went through some emotional pain as she was forced to feel her feelings, but she also discovered that being fully grounded, feet flat on the earth as she walked, nourished her. Mother Earth is a female nurturing energy. When we are linked to the earth, we are safe.

We cannot feel at peace unless our base centre is working properly. When it is we radiate such a sense of peace that others around us feel safe.

When our base centre is active and flowing our work becomes a creative delight. We feel stable and secure. We are immensely powerful peace generators.

CHAPTER 14

Dealing with Emotions and Sexuality

When we evolved from instinctual animals into human beings, we became social beings. We developed the sacral centre, where we learn to give and receive in relationships.

Recorded in this centre are our attitudes and responses to sex, sin and guilt. We link through this chakra to the collective beliefs in sexuality. There are very few human beings who have this centre completely in balance.

The signs of imbalance

If we eat stodge or sweet stuff when we are a bit upset it indicates that this centre is off balance. It is equally out if we starve ourselves or cannot eat when we are upset.

In the extreme, the obese person stuffs in food as a way to keep unwelcome emotions down, while the anorexic starves herself. One takes in food as a substitute for love. The other starves because she believes she does not deserve

129

love. A bulemic swings between these two extremes, bingeing on food instead of love, then, because she feels bad, guilty and undeserving of love, makes herself sick. Often she alternates this with bouts of starvation. Every bulemic I have seen has beliefs which are sexually unbalanced. They have experienced sexual inappropriateness in their childhood and taken on board conflicting messages about sexuality.

If this centre is too yang we may indulge in too much sex for our nature. If it is too yin we may be impotent, frigid or withholding.

The sacral centre is governed by water, which is the emotional element. When we relax and balance this chakra it helps the bladder and bowels, the sexual organs and therefore pre-menstrual tension or menopausal problems.

Negative emotions flow out of our body in our urine. If we are pissed off with someone, usually our partner, then we have more negative emotions than we can release in our urine and may give ourselves a bladder infection. Holding negative emotions over a long period of time can result in kidney problems.

The psychic sensor

The psychic energy of this chakra is clairsentience. It is from here that we send out feelers to sense someone else's pain. If we are open we may take their pain into our body. It will surely help them physically, but we have to deal with their illness, which is their learning and is not appropriate for us to carry. It is the spiritual equivalent of doing our child's homework for him.

Many nice, kind souls amongst us operate with this

chakra open. This is the sort of thing that happens. We meet a friend for a chat and they complain about their awful headache. We listen to their problem and sympathize. They go home better and we go home with the headache! Our sacral chakra reached out and drew in their pain.

I had a nasty experience once which shook me and taught me not to be so open. One lunchtime, as I closed the door behind my last client of the morning, I felt a searing pain go up inside my vagina like a sword being thrust into me. It was agony. I went to the loo and discovered I was bleeding.

A friend arrived for lunch. She made me sit down and gave me a metamorphic treatment on my feet which helped greatly. Somehow I got through the afternoon, trying to relax through the waves of pain. As my last client left, the phone rang. It was a lady I had met only once some weeks before. 'What's the matter?' she asked. 'You're sending out psychic cries for help.' I explained about the sudden terrible pain and bleeding. She promptly suggested that I sit back and she would send me some healing. I sat back in the chair, and as I started to receive the healing energy, I immediately became aware, 'It's not my pain,' I said, 'I've just remembered. A friend is having a cervical cancer operation today.'

As soon as I had that awareness the pain stopped instantly. So did the bleeding.

I realized that I had sent my friend a few healing thoughts in the morning. I had not consciously thought about her since, but my open sacral chakra had picked up her pain and taken it in. When I telephoned her I discovered, needless to say, she was in the operating theatre at the exact time that I felt the knife plunge in. 'I had a very easy time. Hardly any discomfort at all,' she said to me brightly when I told her. 'Thanks very much for taking on my pain. It was a great help.'

Many people heal with the powerful sexual energy of this centre. Orange is the sacral colour and healers who do not have orange in their spectrum get very easily depleted.

Collective beliefs

Humankind's beliefs about sexuality are held in the collective unconscious. We link into those beliefs through our sacral chakra where we hold our individual beliefs about sex.

Our aim in all matters is to separate ourselves from the collective belief, rise above it and align to the Divine wisdom.

In the Divine Mind every individual is held as whole, happy and healthy. In the Divine Mind sex is a pure and beautiful way of two souls merging to raise their energies to a Higher Level and to bring a new soul into creation.

This is what came through to me when I was channelling some information about early Atlantis.

'The Atlanteans had emotions but their chakras were clear and free flowing. The sexual act was beautiful in a way that is incomprehensible now. It was ecstasy but a gentle ecstasy and joining of two souls.

'Before a new soul entered the physical realm, the parents communicated with the spirit. So sex was a way of them connecting with that soul. The energy produced by sexual union linked to the chosen soul and drew him into their vibration to prepare for incarnation. Birth was always a time for rejoicing. The new soul came in for growth and service.'

We all have the capacity to enjoy sex and to bring souls into incarnation in this way. However the collective belief about sex is riddled with guilt and a belief that it is bad and must somehow be subdued. Our beliefs attract us to a religion. If our consciousness holds sexual guilt, we will be attracted to a puritanical or punitive dogma.

When we fantasize sexually about someone, especially if we put energy into that fantasy, we can enter that person's sacral chakra and damage it. They may then have problems in this area. Marilyn Monroe is a classic example of someone who was open to assault from the sexual thoughts of many men. I believe this contributed to her problems and eventual suicide. Of course, in order to allow this assault to affect her she had to be receptive and vulnerable in this area.

In its purest form sexuality is the creative expression of love, which links the masculine and feminine. When our sexual channels are open, the kundalini will rise through the chakras as we orgasm and set fire to all the cells of the body, raising our energy to the spiritual levels. Anger and fear are the greatest blocks to the raising of kundalini energy during sex and very few people in the western world ever achieve true fulfilment.

For many lifetimes non-conforming sexual feelings had to be denied or kept secret where they formed part of our shadow. Many people have brought forward these sexually imperfect beliefs to deal with in this life when there is a climate permitting non-conforming feelings to be expressed.

There are many men and women who are born gay, who have brought that thread through at this time to explore. Others are confused about their gender and are experiencing that confusion in bisexual relationships. One reason for this is that more evolved souls are coming into incarnation. Younger souls will choose a gender with which they feel comfortable. They may have had many lives in a male body or consecutive lives in a female body. As our souls evolve we choose conditions and circumstances which challenge us, so we choose to experience the gender with which we are less familiar.

The roots of sexual confusion

With broken homes, loss of community, isolated living and angry, confused parents, many men are not quite making the switch from identification with mother in childhood to becoming a male who relates back to women. They are stuck in between, settling for a homosexual relationship which is less complex than one with the opposite sex.

It is generally less difficult for a girl who identifies with her mother at birth and watches from there how to relate to a man. Yet many women are turning to lesbian relationships. Often this has nothing to do with sexuality. It is to do with their need to find the nurturing mother they longed for in childhood. They don't find it in a man, so they search for it in a woman.

If our mother did not nurture or support us we will be constantly looking for that emotional energy from our partners. We will try to make our partner meet our nurturing needs.

If our father was not there for us because he was unsupportive, alcoholic, workaholic or in some way absent, we will keep looking for a strong supportive male and will try to make our partner our strong support. We will probably choose an absent partner and try to change him to be the way we imagine our ideal father figure.

Madge was a typical example. She had a frigid, unaware, unnurturing mother who was extremely charming on the surface and full of passive anger underneath. Her father was an immature workaholic, as she described him, who was emotionally absent and unsupportive. Her mother put up with him for years but finally asked him to leave when Madge was in her teens.

In her search for love to support her and fill her emptiness, Madge married young. Inevitably she married a man who was unaware, distant and unable to nurture. Business trips and long hours at work rendered him an absent father to her children. When the oldest child was twelve, Madge went for counselling. Soon after that she found the courage within herself to leave him.

After that she had one short term relationship after another, all with unaware, unnurturing men. She was bemused and angry that she kept attracting the same type of blocked man into her life. However, it was not surprising for, although she was very aware, she was still incredibly angry with men and would not take responsibility for nourishing herself. Her constant cry was, 'They don't meet my needs.'

When she finally found a stable, emotionally nurturing and happy relationship, it was with a woman. She started to look younger and more contented than I had ever seen her before. She was not basically a lesbian but a lesbian relationship met her nurturing needs.

Many of us have tangled beliefs about our sexuality. In our minds we substitute sex for power or money or love or control. I saw a car sticker which said 'I'm looking for love but I'll settle for sex.' That's really sad and yet it is what a lot of us do.

135

Some people put all their sexual energy into the thrill of the chase. They have a wonderful sex life until the point of marriage or living together and then the chase is over. The passion dies and they put their energy elsewhere.

Others sense that if their sex life is not good there is nothing else to hold the relationship together, so they put everything into sexually attracting and holding their partner. When the relationship collapses, as it inevitably does because sex is not a good foundation, they are devastated. They cry, 'I can't understand why it ended. We had such a fantastic sex life.'

Sexual compulsions

Janey felt uncomfortable about the fat she was putting on over her tummy and hips. She was uncomfortable about her sexuality or her ability to give and receive emotionally and the fat protected her.

While she had been having a 'harmless flirtation' with a man for some months she had been as slender as usual. But then he moved away and she had started to put the fat on.

Janey had never felt validated by her father as a little girl, so she constantly looked to men to reassure her that she was attractive. Typically she had married a man very similar to her father, who was hard working, a good provider but had no idea how to help her feel attractive. So Janey had lots of mini flirtations with men, which gave her a thrill, yet were safe.

She admitted that she found her husband boring and did not really want to have sex with him. She just persuaded herself it was O.K.

So when her sexual energy was free flowing in the

excitement of a flirtation, making her feel desirable as a woman, she was slim. When that same energy got stuck with the frustration of a husband who did not make her feel attractive, she put on weight.

Patterns vary. Patricia put on weight at puberty as had her mother. It took a lot of patience to bring to light the denied sexuality. At some level she wanted to be sexual but it was too dangerous, so she put on fat instead.

Addictions, whether to food, sex, drugs, gambling, or spending money, are caused by an imbalance in the sacral centre. They are compulsive behaviours which prevent us feeling our empty feelings and to heal them we need to become a wise supportive parent to the hurting child within.

Stored memories

In the sacral chakra we hold hereditary information. If our great-great-great-grandfather had TB and we carry that gene, we will hold a TB miasm in this centre. This will mean a physical tendency towards TB as well as a tubercular personality. These are often the hollow chested, anxious, non-assertive people.

So many of our ancestors had syphilis, gonorrhoea, cholera, rickets, malaria, insanity, melancholia, amongst countless other diseases, that most of us carry one or more of these tendencies in our sacral centre.

We inherit our predispositions just as when we move to a new house we inherit the garden. The soil may be rich and fertile but it may be tainted. It is tainted soil from which all diseases grow.

What has happened as medical science has found ways of

treating the symptoms without dealing with the cause is this. The disease has seemingly cleared but it is merely suppressed and the sick person still holds the old beliefs and tendencies within his cellular genetic memory. It emerges later down the blood line as a vulnerability to AIDS or cancer or something equally devastating. Many believe that AIDS is mutated syphilis.

A healer friend with X-ray vision who sees miasms in the auric field and in the body told me this story. A patient of hers had bad eczema and she saw in the auric field that the source was a TB miasm two generations back. Homeopathic remedies cleared the eczema and the miasm. It is interesting that TB is associated with milk. People with eczema often complain that dairy products aggravate it.

Eczema can also be the residual physical symptom of a syphilis miasm, as can mucus forming tendencies. There are of course other sources to both eczema and mucus forming tendencies.

Many souls who are bringing these diseases forward now are doing some sort of personal development work to resolve the cause. This is an offering on their part to clear the miasm for the whole family. Then the gene is carried no further. Those of us who do this are healing our ancestors as well as future generations.

There is so much willing help available for any of us wanting healing. We can invoke the help of ancestors, spirit guides, angels, avatars, Christ, Buddha or God and we will be guided and sustained on our Path of Inner Peace.

CHAPTER 15

Claiming Our Power

The solar plexus chakra is governed by the fire element. It is yellow—pale yellow if we are cowardly, sunny buttercup yellow if we are strong. If we are wise, it has a golden quality.

With a strong solar plexus, no one can influence us or disempower us. We are confident and have a sense of personal value and worth. It is the seat of the lower will which has to be mastered before we can let go of self and move to higher service.

The threat detector

It is through this centre that we pick up information about danger around us. It sends out fingers of psychic energy which sense what is going on with people and situations that affect us. So if we are driving down a motorway this centre sends out feelers to check that all is safe. It is here that we form our impressions of business deals, have an uneasy feeling that someone we love is in trouble or get the message not to go into a particular street or house.

Most of us have one predominant way of absorbing information. One person will be primarily visual, another learns by hearing and a third by touch. In the same way one will psychically sense his surroundings through the solar plexus while another will psychically see what is happening with his third eye.

Just as we form an overall impression of someone with our physical senses by seeing them, hearing their voice, touching them, smelling and tasting their scent, we similarly form overall psychic impressions. Through the sacral centre we will feel their feelings, while through the solar plexus we will sense whether or not we are safe with them. Our heart centre will warn us if we will be hurt or if we can open to love them. Through our throat centre we will 'hear' our inner voice guiding us. Information gathered through our third eye may come as pictures for we will be seeing into or around that person's life. This is the level of intuition, where we use our inner wisdom, so we will have certainty about it, rather than the uneasy sensing quality of the lower chakras.

How we interpret this information depends on the fears we hold here and we deal with the input according to the strength of our chakra.

This is our personal power centre. When we are self confident, brave and have a sense of self-worth, this centre will be strong and we will be powerful. In this case, shocks, other people's rage directed at us, even a vehicle screeching to a stop and just missing us, will not affect us.

If this centre is weak or vulnerable for some reason and someone verbally attacks us, their shaft of anger can split our centre open, like a bullet smashing into a target. The reason most of us cannot cope with very angry people is because our solar plexus centre is too sensitive. It tenses up or collapses under threat.

When we are given bad news the shock is usually absorbed here.

If we are very sensitive we tune into universal happenings through this chakra. So the antennae in our solar plexus can pick up the danger of an earthquake the other end of the world, causing us to tense up without consciously knowing why.

Many people operate on this level without quite understanding what is happening. I talked to a young mother who woke up one morning just knowing she was not going to take her children to school that day. She was not sure why. It just felt dangerous. So she kept them at home. At lunchtime she heard on the news that a gunman had killed a number of children in a school. It was at the other end of the world but she knew inside that the danger she had picked up was past and she took her children back to school in the afternoon.

The physical signs of imbalance

On a physical level, this centre covers the stomach, liver, gall bladder, pancreas. So, if we sense danger through this chakra and our tummy tightens up we have difficulty digesting food. This is symbolic of the fact that we cannot digest the experience which we sense around us.

When we suppress primitive emotions, especially aggression, we hold it in our liver. So if someone shouts at us so vehemently that their anger energy penetrates our chakra, our own suppressed anger will be shaken up. This is why we feel so bad and often we close down even more tightly.

As ever it indicates that we need to look at emotions we have not dealt with.

After a shock people often cannot eat because this centre has been paralyzed and the stomach cannot send out digestive juices.

If we feel angry with others or the world situation or the inhumanity of humankind and we feel powerless to do anything about it, then we internalize that anger. Cancers and tumours are physical manifestations of internalized aggression.

Giving away power

When we give away our power, we weaken our solar plexus chakra. These are some of the ways we do it:

1. When we rely on someone else instead of standing on our own two feet.
2. When we look for advice instead of thinking for ourself.
3. When we need approval from another.
4. When we depend on someone for support.
5. When we let someone else take decisions for us.
6. When we sympathize with someone rather than empathize.
7. When we feel the need to rescue someone.
8. When we hang onto people because we cannot cope without them.
9. When we feel guilty or blame others.
10. When we give another permission to hurt us, make us angry etc.
11. When we manipulate instead of asking directly for what we want.

12. When we let ourselves be manipulated.
13. When we try to please others for fear they will not like us if we don't.
14. When we grumble and complain without taking appropriate action.

Some years ago I was chatting over lunch to a friend who was a channeller by profession. Abruptly she paused with her fork in the air and pronounced, 'There's a message for you.' Without pausing for breath, and concentrating intently, she said, 'We would allow your work to move faster if we could trust you to rely on self and not keep running to others for answers.'

I felt like a schoolgirl. I wanted indignantly to deny that I ran to others for answers but I had so many friends who were spiritually attuned that it was easy to say yes when they offered to lay out a deck of tarot or to tune in for guidance, instead of doing it for myself.

There are times when it is helpful, life-changing even, to consult a good channeller or psychic. However if we *keep* running to clairvoyants and counsellors instead of listening to our intuition, we give away our power and weaken our solar plexus chakra.

To become masters of our lives, we are called upon to do our part by working with meditation, intention and self-development to strengthen our own hotline to God. With this connection comes inner safety, peace, wisdom and power.

We may gain important insight and awareness when we work with a therapist or counsellor. We may get fresh viewpoints and a wider perspective when we talk an issue through with colleagues or friends. This is empowering as long as we then *take our own decisions* based on more complete information. However it is letting go of self-responsibility when we run to others for guidance instead of making up our own minds and it must slow our progress on our Path.

The roots of powerlessness

Ian was the oldest of several children, the product of an angry mother and a feckless, sometimes violent father. Three more children, including twins, were born in the next three years and his father walked out when his mother became pregnant again. He vanished, leaving them without maintenance or support of any kind.

She simply could not cope alone, impoverished as she was, with her large brood. Her constant threat to the children was that she would leave. It was the only way she knew of controlling them.

Ian as a sensitive child lived in abject terror that she would abandon them as his father had done. He spent his entire childhood trying to please and placate this angry woman so that she would stay. He believed that when she inevitably did leave he would have to look after the others and he did not know how to.

That alone is a heavy burden for a small child to carry. In addition, his mother controlled her large family with anger, with bursts of violence, by constant criticism and by trying to make them feel bad and guilty. She also sulked and brooded for days, which is a cruel manipulation.

All the controls his mother used damage the power centre if we let them. We in our turn damage our children until we learn to stand up for ourselves.

As an evolved soul, Ian had a great desire to learn the lessons he needed to from his childhood. At a conscious level, he had much insight, higher awareness and great strength and determination to deal with the blocks within him that these lessons represented.

At an inner level Ian had a frozen child within him. Whenever his childhood feelings were triggered, if for instance someone with the same energy as his mother was angry with him, he would become that terrified child and try to placate them. He believed that he was powerless, that there was nothing he could do and at the same time his life depended on stopping them from being angry. Inevitably, he lacked confidence and self-worth. He covered this up by choosing a career where others depended on him to look after them and he put his all into being very good at his job and totally indispensable.

In order to carry the burdens of his childhood and, later, his adult responsibilities, he built himself massive shoulders. He also created himself a large well-muscled chest to defend his heart centre. It is not an easy task to let go of such armouring but Ian has evolved as a teacher over many lifetimes. He had great insights as well as much esoteric knowledge and an absolute knowing that he had come into this life to teach the Spiritual Truths. He knew he must heal his childhood pain and fear before he could teach with full conviction.

He did anger release sessions with a bodywork therapist to soften his body armouring. Bit by bit he took the steps necessary to reclaim his power and strengthen his solar plexus. Then he gradually opened his heart centre more and more. He attended many workshops and I watched in delight as his frozen inner child thawed and softened.

I paid particular attention whenever he did a spontaneous drawing of his parents, for our unconscious mind then gives us so much information about the way we parent ourselves. It was enchanting to watch over time as his drawings of his parents became more complete, more flexible and more welcoming, indicating that profound changes were taking place at an unconscious level.

I watched Ian, who had had such a difficult childhood, emerge from a man who constantly had to justify and defend himself, who lacked confidence and was based in his solar plexus, into an independent, gentle, confident heart-centred man.

If we lack confidence and are afraid of our own or other's anger we are operating from our solar plexus. It is time NOW to learn to stand up for ourselves and raise our energy to our heart centre..

The power of the mind

The mind and the solar plexus are linked. The colour of intellect is yellow as is the colour associated with the solar plexus. Libraries are often painted yellow because we instinctively know this is a colour which helps us to study and concentrate. So our thoughts directly affect this chakra.

This is why positive direct suggestions in hypnosis strengthen the solar plexus chakra. There are, of course, many good hypnotherapists whose work strengthens the other chakras too, but simple, positive suggestion in hypnosis empowers this one. I well recall my first experience of hypnosis for it was a changing point in my life.

During the twenty odd years of my first marriage I had consistently given my power away. I had become a nervous wreck as I fought my way through the difficulties of divorce and I was barely coping with life.

I started to train as a hypnotherapist and my teacher

said she would use me as a model for the class and give me a brief session of hypnosis to strengthen me so that I could deal with my difficult situation. She put me into a light trance and built in direct suggestions to the effect that I was calm and strong and would be able to deal with everything in a confident and relaxed way.

I went home feeling I could cope with anything and anyone! For the first time ever none of my husband's anger, nor his comments or threats, affected me. They rolled off me like water off a balloon and I remember thinking, 'You have no power to hurt me.'

He was very much bemused at the total change in me and stopped attacking. What is the point of attacking if there is no reaction! *To feel at peace is an incredibly powerful place to be.*

The next day a speeding, out of control car on the wrong side of the road narrowly missed me and hit the car next to me, seriously injuring the occupants. My heart did not even miss a beat. I felt I could deal with anything.

After a few days the effect of that very brief hypno-therapy session wore off, but I retained the memory of what it was like to feel totally empowered. That imprint sustained me for a long time.

We can only let ourselves be manipulated if we are not clear. When we are clear of who we are, that we have a right to be respected, that no one can touch us without our permission, then we do not allow anyone to manipulate us. So if we are allowing ourselves to be manipulated, then we may need some help to find clarity about our rights.

To be nice to others from a genuine space of love is empowering and comes from being centred in our heart. Too often, however, we please others as a defence mechanism so that we will not be rejected or disliked, and this weakens our solar plexus. The pleaser who has to placate, do-good, rescue and care for others, because she is seeking approval or a sense of worth, is operating on fear, based in the solar plexus. The ultimate pleaser is a martyr, doormat, manipulator or ingratiator. Underneath she is desperately needy. Our need-based desire to be nice to others weakens our solar plexus.

If we have feelings of devastation at the thought of loss, we are operating from our solar plexus. So if the thought of our partner leaving distresses us, if the idea of losing our home, or status or material possessions upsets us, if the thought of losing our job panics us, we need to strengthen our solar plexus.

It is easy to recognize if our pleaser is need-based. When we give our power away to please others, we feel underlying resentment. If we deny this, our body will give us clues, such as arthritis, headaches, cancers, pain.

If we decide to claim our power and decline to please others, our pleaser often makes us feel guilty. Guilt is the flip side of resentment and is that resentment turned inward against ourselves. It comes from a belief we are bad and it disempowers us and stops us from taking responsibility for our lives.

Here are steps we can take to strengthen our solar plexus.

1. Breathing exercises.
2. Tummy exercises.
3. Sunlight on the solar plexus. If there is no sun, the next best thing is to visualize it.
4. Positive affirmations to increase confidence.
5. Take all the small decisions we keep putting off and act on them. Then take the larger ones.

6. Decide what we really want to do and do it.
7. Decide what we want and ask directly for it.
8. If we feel guilty, who or what are we resentful at? What are we going to do or say to change our situation?
9. Uncord ourself from people and things we suspect we are attached to.
10. Make ourself independent.
11. Laughter shakes fear out of our solar plexus.
12. Step-by-step do all the little things we have been scared of doing ourself.

When we claim our power, we are at peace.

CHAPTER 16

Our Heart Knows

In the very core of our being, in the centre of our heart centre, is a strong, safe place. This is where Christ consciousness is held within us. We all have this space, it does not depend on religion or spirituality. It just is.

When we operate from this space, nothing and no one can upset or harm us, we connect to the universal energy of unconditional love.

Opening the heart centre

The colour of the heart chakra is a bright clear green, the link between the yellow of the solar plexus and the blue of the throat centre. The colour of the inner heart is rose pink.

I learnt about the wonder of this rose pink colour and energy in a strange way in my early days in practice. I lived in a small cottage painted pink outside and pale pink inside. In my sitting room I had rose pink curtains and at night I had a lamp with a pink bulb which shone onto the curtains and radiated the most beautiful peaceful light.

However I worked in another room.

My client was a healer, a very spiritual lady, but I felt she had a blockage in her heart chakra. I guided her to explore and she found some darkness and debris in there, which she cleared out. I was about to ask her to open her eyes when an extraordinary thing happened. Suddenly I saw rays of light – a deep rose pink – the exact colour of the light on the sitting room curtains – starting to flow from her heart centre. They were so bright that the colour lit up the room.

I actually got up and walked over to the window to check if someone was outside shining a powerful pink light into the room which by some trick looked as if it was radiating from inside my client!

When I sat down again the bright pink rays were pouring even more strongly from her heart centre and then fingers of light started moving in and out, reaching round the room like the fronds of a sea anemone.

I do not know how long I watched this incredible sight for but when my client opened her eyes I told her in some excitement about what I had seen. She was unaware of what I had been experiencing, but felt very peaceful about the issue we were healing and validated about the quality of the beautiful energy she was releasing.

When we are totally centred in our heart centre we feel so safe that nothing can knock us or frighten us. From this space we are open to our higher guidance.

A safe haven

Beverly phoned me for an emergency appointment. She was panicking and her body was covered in a nervous rash.

'I thought I was coping, and suddenly I feel lost and very frightened,' she said. During her childhood, several members of her family had died. She understood she was learning lessons of detachment in this life but that she was absolutely terrified of losing her husband or children and this fear was preying on her.

For a long time she had wanted to move to a bigger house. Now at last they could afford to do so. Their house was on the market and suddenly she felt very insecure. 'All I want in life is a happy, safe home,' she reiterated again and again. Because Beverly was so shaky, I reminded her that safety is within us and that we all have a sanctuary deep in our heart centre where we can find peace. It is from this sanctuary that we can face our fears and see them for the illusions they are.

One way of reaching this safe haven within us is to visualize a sanctuary inside ourselves which we can visit whenever we need to find inner peace or answers to our problems.

I asked Beverly where she would feel safe and she told me she would need to be in a small sitting room with a thick carpet, a sofa and a log fire. Then I helped her to relax into a receptive state and gave her time to create her safe sitting room. When she could sense it clearly, she imagined herself walking round the room stroking the soft velvet of the sofa, feeling the texture of the wallpaper and touching the cool stone of the hearth. Then she listened to the sound of the grandfather clock ticking in the corner and heard the crackle of the flames in the fireplace. Lastly she smelt the furniture polish, the pine cones on the wood fire and the fragrant flowers in a bowl on a low table.

By now she was feeling very relaxed and secure. She knew that no fear could influence her while she was in this safe place. So I suggested that one of her great fears was knocking on the door and it was time to face it. She opened the door and saw Death standing there. It looked like a skeleton.

'What are you doing here?' she asked.

I asked her what Death replied. 'He's saying, "I came to remind you that death is just a transition. Remember what to the caterpillar is death to the butterfly is life."' Beverly thanked the messenger and relaxed visibly.

'I'm not afraid of you any more, Death,' she said in a surprisingly strong clear voice. She saw the skeleton vanish and felt her fear dissolve. Then she closed the door and once more enjoyed the peace and tranquillity of her inner sanctum.

The next time fear knocked on the door, she opened it to several thin, grey ghost-like creatures. 'We're loneliness,' they told her.

'What do you want from me?'

'Love. Please love us.'

Suddenly she saw that they represented all the people around her who wanted to be loved! All she had to do was open her heart and let them all in. Then she would never be lonely again.

She began to laugh uproariously. 'They've turned into people,' she gasped with laughter, her whole body shaking as she laughed and laughed. I watched the fear being shaken out of her. When she stopped laughing her face was beaming. 'I want to invite them in,' she said. 'I need never fear loneliness again.' When she opened her eyes, the fear had left them.

Fear is a servant bringing a message. It has no power over us. The messenger is not powerful, only the impact of the message.

We can all create ourselves an inner sanctuary. It does

not matter where it is. We can imagine a room, a meadow in the country or be by the sea. We can be anywhere. The only important point is that we create a place where we feel safe and at peace.

From our inner haven of peace we are totally powerful. When we look at fear from this perspective we recognize it as the illusion it is.

Guidance from nature

It is not by chance that green, which is nature's colour, is the colour of the heart centre.

Unconditional love is non-judgmental. Nature is non-judgmental. So when we are in the heart of nature we feel safe. When we relax into this safety, we can more readily hear the promptings of our Higher Self.

When we need guidance we can ask our question and go out into nature and be sure that our answer will be given to us in some form.

When I run week workshops I sometimes ask the participants to formulate a question to which they desire an answer. Then I suggest they go for a walk in nature and look for the answer, knowing that it will be given to them in some way.

One lady was very unfulfilled and unsupported in her marriage. For years she had longed to leave her partner but feared the impact it would have on her children. She posed the question, 'Shall I leave?' She found herself walking along an isolated path where she noticed a holly tree. One side of the tree was black and withered, the other was alive and full of berries. As she observed this she saw a squirrel with a baby in its mouth. The squirrel paused in front of her as if to draw her attention to what it was doing. She saw that it had a baby in its mouth and realized that the squirrel was moving its babies from one nest to another. She knew the babies would be safe in their new nest. Nature was gathering its forces to give her a response to her question.

A man who kept getting stuck in his business ventures asked just how far he should go in the new one. It felt right to him but he doubted because of his past experiences.

He began to walk along a path tangled with undergrowth and brambles. Just as he was deciding to go back he came out into a clearing which opened onto sand and sea. The sea met the blue sky and there were no barriers. The words came into his head. 'There are no barriers. The sky's the limit.' When he went home he put his heart into his new venture.

Unconditional love

When we so love another that we are one with them, we automatically heal them. Oneness is a state of Grace. It only takes a moment and we cannot will it. The person may be a stranger or a loved one. In this state of Love we are so aligned with our Divine Self that we raise the other person's consciousness to God and miracles take place. We do not have to wait for a God force outside ourselves to grant Grace. When we feel unconditional love it touches the heart centre of another and kindles the Divine spark within them.

The lesson of the heart centre is unconditional love. This means accepting the other person exactly as they are. It is the highest lesson in relationships and implies total detachment. It means accepting that what another person chooses to do on his learning path cannot hurt or diminish us in any way.

I was once staying at an ashram in India. Here I was feeling very loving and spiritually attuned. When we ask for a lesson we always get it and I dared to ask to learn the lesson of Unconditional Love. That night I found myself sleeping in a shed with 300 women and I swear 299 of them snored! As I lay there trying to sleep through the noise, tossing and turning, with my fingers in my ears, I realized how far from unconditionally loving I was.

Some of us put ourselves through very difficult relationships in order to learn this very high form of love. *If someone is sweet and loving to us, it is no test.* If we are evolved beings and we choose parents, family or life conditions which are very cruel or demanding, we are giving ourselves opportunities to open our heart centre.

Helen had a mother who was a manic depressive. Throughout her childhood, Helen's Mother had been irresponsible, irrational, inconsistent, demanding and often rejecting. The child never knew how she would be and took early decisions to be independent and never rely on anyone. She firmly closed down her heart centre to her mother.

By the time Helen reached her fifties she was warm, wise and was blossoming into an incredible spiritual teacher. Despite her awareness, she found it difficult to open her heart to her very difficult, demanding old mother who was by now in her late seventies.

One day in meditation Helen connected with the fact that her mother was a very beautiful and evolved soul who had offered to come into this life with mental problems specifically to give her daughter the difficult test she needed. She offered to live a frightened and lonely existence to offer Helen the opportunity of undergoing an Earth Plane examination in unconditional love.

It was after that inner awareness that Helen began to make subtle shifts which opened her heart centre.

So often we find that our worst enemy at a personality level is our greatest friend at a spiritual level and they may even have stepped off their pathway especially to help us learn a lesson.

Unconditional love is truly that. When we love unconditionally we say, 'I accept you as you are.' In order to have my love there are no conditions on the way you behave. I love you even though you appear to hate me. I love you even though you have left all your money to my brother. I love you even though you desert me.

When we unconditionally love ourselves we are very clear about who we are and how we are prepared to be treated. Unconditionally loving someone does not mean that we must live with them. If we have outgrown the relationship it may no longer serve our Path or theirs to live with them. We still accept and love them as they are. It is perfectly consistent to say. 'I love you as you are. And as I love myself too, I no longer wish to live with you.'

We all have a twin soul who is the other half of our soul, our perfect partner. Most of us have a faint memory of this and yearn at a deep unconscious level to come together again. However, on Planet Earth we evolve through experiences and tests, not by being spoon fed, so to be with our twin soul is not a growth relationship. Our twin soul may not even be incarnate at the same time as we are. However we will meet again one day.

When we open our hearts, we are part of the oneness of the Universe. We are one with animals and all nature. We feel ourselves part of the eternal cosmic heartbeat. We are in a state of Inner Peace.

CHAPTER 17

The Power of Truth

The throat centre is one of the most sensitive and fragile chakras in our body. The lesson here is honesty of communication. In order for this centre to be working perfectly we must be totally in touch with our feelings and be able to declare them. At the same time we must be able to listen to the voice of our Higher Self and communicate this too with honesty to others. This implies a complete trust in the spiritual guidance we receive. By the time we are opening this centre we must have the integrity to follow our truth.

Holding back the truth

When people are opening up spiritually this is the centre which tends to cause problems. We are taught in childhood to please and placate others, which often involves being dishonest. We continue with this pattern because it feels safer than dealing with the imagined consequences of our honesty.

When we please and placate, we are serving the other

person's personality self, not their soul. At the same time we clog our throat centre with untruths. If we fear that what we want to say will not be heard openly and lovingly, our throat centre tightens.

If we are angry or afraid and dare not express ourself openly, our throat tenses up. If we are so angry that we may say something which will have dangerous consequences for us, our unconscious mind may make our voice disappear. When we lose our voice, we cannot say what we want to.

As higher dimensional beings we are called on to walk our Truth without the need of approval or acceptance from others.

When we speak our truth with honesty and integrity our throat centre opens and we are heard by those who are ready to hear.

Other people's truth

If for any reason we feel under threat, we may find that the back of our throat centre tightens up. Then we have a stiff neck. This may be because our ideas are being challenged or perhaps others disagree with us. Perhaps we feel out of control or unable to speak out. Our task is to become more flexible and open. We may need to become more accepting of other people's view or opinions. We do not need to let go of our own truths.

When we open up to the higher spiritual truths our light inevitably draws darker souls, those of lesser understanding, who may deride or challenge us. When we are knocked off-centre by this we empower the lesser understanding. When we stay strong, honest and true we subtly raise others to the truth.

As we communicate with honesty and integrity, the turquoise blue of this centre becomes clearer and deeper.

When we constantly study and absorb other people's ideas we rust up this centre and stop it from spinning. My daughter is very sensitive and spiritual. When she left university she was plagued with sore throats. She was told that her throat centre was clogged up with all the opinions of other people that she had had to quote for her thesis. She needed space in order to let go of others' truths. Only then could she attune once more to her own knowing and bring her own original thoughts and ideas through. She realized the sense of this and relaxed. Over the next three months the sore throats gradually disappeared.

Our education system at every level emphasizes learning from books and reading other people's work. No essay is considered complete unless it quotes other people's thoughts. This clogs our throat centre. Original and creative thinking opens and expands it.

Singing and chanting are wonderful ways of cleansing and opening this centre. Sing in the bath. Chant as you drive. Hum as you walk. Open up to the higher energies of Truth and Trust.

One of the most powerful ways of healing our throat centre is honestly to share our feelings with people we trust and have them lovingly honoured.

Trusting our authentic feelings

Our throat chakra is our trust centre and incredible healings take place when we trust others enough to speak out our deep dark secrets in a group. When we find ourselves still loved and accepted it is as if an exorcism has taken place.

A group will rarely hurt or reject anyone who lets

themselves be genuinely vulnerable and honest. However bad the deed or dreadful the experience, when we share our honest feelings, the group will enfold us in loving care and support us long after the group has broken up.

Occasionally someone shares a deep hurt or trauma but instead of coming from a genuine feeling space, they disassociate from the emotions and come from their heads. A group's antennae become very sensitive. When this happens the collective feeling is usually one of resentment. The group feels conned. I remember one workshop where a number of participants had shared deeply emotional and traumatic hurts. They received such love and empathy from the group that the bonding was very close.

Only Gladys stood apart. No one felt close to her although she was always the first to put her arms round people, to say loving things to them and do things for them. However, it came from a space of need. She was a rescuer who desperately needed people to love her. All her life she had found that people were irritated or annoyed with her and she had no idea why. So she compulsively tried to please others.

Gladys had had a heartbreaking childhood and painful adulthood. It was not surprising that she was so needy. She kept claiming group time to talk about her awful experiences. Every time she shared, it came from her head not from her heart. She did not trust the group with her feelings and the group stood back from her. No one rescued her. She could not understand why everyone else got loved and nurtured after they shared and she did not.

With enormous integrity each person in the group gave Gladys feedback about their feelings of frustration and irritation. Gladys was devastated. For the first time she connected totally with the overpowering, out-of-control, hurting, angry space inside herself. That space had been there since childhood and she had been trying to protect herself from feeling it. She rescued other people from feeling their grief and hurt so that she would not have to feel her own. Now she cried tears of grief and rage as she shared her genuine feelings. And the group loved her and rocked her, held her and soothed her. Possibly for the first time in her life, she felt truly loved and safe and accepted.

When we express our honest feelings we receive a loving response.

The trust centre

The throat chakra is known as the will centre or the trust centre. Here we learn to listen to and trust our inner voice. It is the centre of clairaudience.

We can also pick up other people's thoughts here as well as at the third eye. If we are unwilling to receive these thoughts, in other words we do not like what people are thinking about us, we may find we need to clear our throat or get a sore throat!

If in another life we have been hanged, executed, strangled or received some injury to this centre we are very likely to bring into this life issues around trust. The cells in our throat centre will retain the ancient memory of the violation and our emotions around it.

Jean carried her head at a slight angle and constantly had neck aches. She also had a very difficult relationship with her father in this life. During a past-life regression she threw herself onto the floor and lay inert with her head at a most peculiar angle. She could not speak for some time because she was going through some deep inner work she could not express.

When she could speak again she told me that she had been a young girl from a rich Parisian family, very happy, engaged to be married and she had been imprisoned and guillotined. The man who had been her executioner in that life was now her father.

She re-entered that life and expressed the violation and rage that she had felt but could not express. She met the personality who had been her executioner then. In her inner world she talked to him and got some understanding of his frustration, rage and fear that his family was starving while the rich were living with plenty. She humbly begged his pardon for her total thoughtlessness. He begged her forgiveness for what he had done.

From that regression she brought into this life more compassion, a sense of understanding for her father, more ability to communicate honest feelings, greater trust towards men and a marked improvement in her neck pain.

A fear of failure may manifest as a blockage in the throat centre for it is a belief that we cannot trust ourself.

May felt as if a block was stopping her from moving forward in life. She felt guilty without any reason and terrified of doing new things because she might fail. All the tension in her body was held in her neck and solar plexus. She had endless colds and sore throats and was always clearing her throat.

When she was nine years old she had been hit in the back of the neck in a freak accident by a swinging bar. As she talked about this she made a chopping motion with her hand. She had had a pain at this point in her neck ever since.

I asked her to close her eyes and focus on the pain in her neck. She became a child of seven years old, crying and terrified. She had failed her exams at school and her father was angry and shouting. 'He says they will have to move house because of me,' she sobbed. 'It's because I'm no good. I'm a failure.'

I introduced her to the concept of a wise parent and asked one of her wise parents to come in and speak to the child. A wise father came into her inner scene. He loved and reassured the child, offered her help and praise for her good points and told her that she had only failed because she was so tense. He told her that she was a clever little girl really and reminded her of many times when she had done well. He also told her that they were moving house because of Daddy's work and it coincided with her failing the exam.

As she heard the wise father remind her of these things, many of which she was not consciously aware of, May looked considerably more relaxed.

She then slipped spontaneously into a past life where she had been a small boy. The little boy had no parents, only two sisters. They were all starving and had to steal to survive. He was caught stealing a loaf of bread. He was thrown into prison and eventually hanged.

He felt a failure because he was caught. As he died he felt he could not trust anyone. He felt that somehow he must be a terrible person to have such an awful thing happen to him.

I asked him to go into the Universe and find that hangman and the man who had sentenced him to die. He connected with them and very clearly communicated his feelings. He also saw how they mirrored his fear. He was afraid of having nothing. They were afraid of having everything taken away. As he saw that they were all acting from the same fear he found understanding and compassion within himself.

Just bringing this awareness to consciousness and expressing the hurt allowed a shift to take place within May. She reported back that she felt calmer, more confident in herself and was able to talk to people much more easily. At another level she became aware that the bar hitting her in the neck was no accident and accepted more fully the knowing that there is no such thing as an accident. Everything happens in response to our energies.

Solutions through self-expression

There is a solution to every problem. At a personality level on the Earth Plane we may not be able to see this. We think there is no answer for us, no way out of our impossible situation. As spiritual beings, using the Universal Laws, all things are possible.

Felicity came to me because she could not have sex with her boyfriend. They had been together for two years and she had had a brief sexual relationship before. She told me she loved him and wanted to have a full relationship with him but when he came near her she went rigid.

It transpired that they were living with his mother who was slightly disabled and very possessive. The mother was afraid of the dark, afraid of being alone and would never let them go away for a night. Felicity's partner adored his mother and did everything for her but she told me that his brother would not stay with their Mum even for a night.

Felicity was angry and frustrated. It was no wonder that she was not able to express love for her partner. When we feel angry, we block our sexuality. However, she had not even registered that she was deeply angry.

She could not see any way of changing the situation. They could not afford to buy a place of their own. Even if they could, her boyfriend's mother could not manage on her own and was terrified of being alone. What is more, she had no money so she couldn't live without her son's contribution.

Felicity believed she was stuck in an impossible situation. I explained to her that we are incredibly powerful people and we write our own scripts. I told her that as long as she believed she was stuck and sent messages out to the Universe of anger and helplessness, nothing would change. All the time she focused on angry pictures of the stuck situation the Universal energy would support her pictures.

I explained that we must picture what we do want and picture happy outcomes for everyone, for the Universe supports our pictures quite impersonally. So she created a picture of herself and her boyfriend living together on their own. At the same time she visualized her partner's mother, relaxed, safe and happy, surrounded by loving people. Because she felt the situation was hopeless, she had never really expressed what she felt to anyone, not even her boyfriend. She swallowed down the feelings, clogging her throat centre, and dealt with everything in a passively angry way which kept her body in tension so that she could not express love.

Now she went home with an energy of expectancy, of hope. She told her boyfriend how she felt. He had never realized that this sweet, compliant woman he lived with had strong feelings. It galvanized him into speaking to his mother and his brother, not with anger but with clarity.

Because he did not talk angrily but made it clear that he wanted a change, they heard and understood.

When we are clear about our feelings and have the courage to be honest we reclaim our power and are heard and understood.

Felicity kept up her vision of living alone with her boyfriend while his mother was being cared for and supported in a loving environment. The Universe started to support the girl's new energy. She phoned me in great excitement and amazement to say that her boyfriend's brother had a house which had been on the market for ages and which he could not sell. He had offered it to them cheaply. They had done their sums and they could afford it. She was over the moon.

Things started to move quickly. Social services agreed to pay the mother's rent. Now that they were communicating with the brother and including him in the family consultations, he felt warmer and more friendly towards them all. He offered to spend two nights a week with his mother. She was delighted because she could feel closer to him again. Neighbours, friends, other relatives rallied round in a most incredible way. The mother was finding her world opening up.

Felicity and her partner did not want to get married until they knew they could have a physical relationship. It felt like a catch 22 situation again. It was clear that her negative inner parent was giving the girl a very hard time about sex outside marriage.

All answers lie within our own consciousness. She closed her eyes and brought in a very wise mother to guide her. This wise mother suggested that they could have their own private ceremony with a ritual where they pledged themselves to each other. Then they could go away for a few days to be completely alone together. She felt very excited by this idea and her partner agreed with it. A friend offered them a caravan by the sea to stay in. Alone together for the first time, they were able to consummate their relationship. She has consistently sent me cards ever since to say that she cannot believe the miracle that has taken place.

Miracles happen when we listen to our inner wisdom and follow our truth.

Our personality self may not be able to find an answer to our problem but to the Universal Wisdom all things are possible.

The throat centre is where we assimilate our lessons. This means integrating all the split off parts of our personality. Then we can act with integrity and heal our throat chakra.

When Felicity communicated her feelings she integrated part of her angry and powerless inner child.

When May accepted her seven-year-old who had failed, she re-integrated her failure personality.

When Jean forgave her executioner father, she re-integrated the part of herself that feared all could be taken from her.

With integration comes a sense of peace.

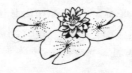

CHAPTER 18

Opening
to Inspiration

When we are ready to open the third eye we are no longer interested in our own individual little self. We are tuned to the cosmic vision. This centre is in the centre of the forehead between and above the physical eyes. It is a centre of great power and beauty, traditionally a deep indigo blue.

This is the centre of clairvoyance, which is clear seeing with the inner spiritual vision. This is a much prized psychic gift and many people strive to open the third eye in isolation which is not good or helpful to the development of the soul. It is a finely attuned and delicate centre. Through it come not only clear sight, but various levels of telepathy, intuition and knowing.

Serving others

The dance of the seven veils was performed throughout the Arabian culture, symbolically indicating the opening of our third eye, layer by layer. At each level of our growth what we see is illusory. In the mystic tradition, the removal of each veil symbolized the lifting of a level of illusion. It is only when the last veil is removed that we drop the separation of ego and move into all revealing oneness. Then we see with the clarity of enlightenment.

Another analogy would be the opening of one door at a time to the wisdom of our soul and to our link with the cosmos. The journey through these doors to cosmic consciousness is one of focus, concentration, meditation, visualization and service. Loving service is one key to opening a door to the third eye. When our heart centre is open and loving, our throat centre is open to truth, then our third eye can open to service.

I was returning from India. On the plane I sat next to a lady who had been doing health work in the slums of Bombay and in remote villages. She told me that their biggest problem was that parents would not bring their sick children to the clinic for help.

In one instance a child had pus pouring from an ear infection and was in considerable pain. The parents said that the child had brought it upon itself. It was the child's karma.

Of course, on one level that is true. We create everything that happens to us by our beliefs which inevitably attracts our karma to us. However, parents will usually so love a child that they will seek appropriate help for the child. Their loving concern is the intercession which brings grace and dissolves the child's karma.

A young woman told me she was born with a badly deformed foot. It was twisted almost backwards in the womb and her family was told by the doctors that she would never walk. But her grandfather would not accept that verdict. He spent hours every day massaging her foot until it gradually became straight and she could walk. His unselfish, loving devotion bestowed grace upon her.

We can't all do great things but we can all do small things in a great way.

Loving others so much that we want to serve them opens up our own chakras. This is not something we can artificially force. It is something that happens when the energy is right.

Releasing planetary karma

The third eye is the chakra of inspiration, aspiration, good intention and universal love. At this level we find liberation because we know there is no limitation and no separation. Here we truly experience oneness so we serve the planet and the cosmos. We heal others and dissolve their karma.

It is not only individuals who have karma but families, group souls, nations and planets do too. When our third eye is open properly and we have overall vision, we have the power and wisdom to release the accumulated karma of others. This is what Christ referred to when he said he could wash away the sins of the world.

As Planet Earth is in the process of moving to a higher level of consciousness, the vibrations of all who choose to remain must rise. We are to become a planet of Grace so there will be no more karma. It is time to transmute our own karma and that of others. Karma can be dissolved by Grace, which is pure unconditional love and oneness. We do not have to wait for God to dissolve someone's karma. Our essence is Divine and when we awaken our third eye we have enough of our Divine essence available to be able to bestow the gift of Grace.

Whenever we forgive another we offer them Grace.

When we open the third eye we can offer this Grace to humanity. We are operating from our Divine self.

The sooner all karma is dissolved the sooner Planet Earth can take its rightful place in the heavens and become a transmitter of Light.

It is as if the Earth has been a lighted globe dropped in the mud. The mud has covered the globe and permeated it, putting the light out. Now we are to be washed, cleansed, purified and the light relit. Then we are to be realigned to the cosmic forces and replaced in our important position in the Universe.

Imagine an intricate pattern of lights, linked in a special way to radiate a message. The lights shine out bright and clear but one bulb has gone out and it is a strategic one which brings the whole pattern together. That is the importance of Planet Earth. The work we do to open and light ourselves up affects our planet and therefore the whole Universe.

Anyone who is not ready to participate in the Age of Grace will not be able to reincarnate on Planet Earth but will be able to have a physical experience in a body on another planet where there is still karma.

The power of vision

When the third eye centre is balanced and open we have enormous powers of focused concentration. This can be used like a laser beam to penetrate the darkness. It can be used to incise the hurts of humankind. It can be used to focus light onto a person or situation. It is as if a beam of light pours out from our third eye to do this work.

The indigo blue of this centre is a mental healing

colour. It can be radiated out to enfold people who are hurt or disturbed in a cocoon of safety and then to stroke and soothe their minds. When we focus on a person or situation and visualize them whole or happy in light, then we are using this centre.

One way of opening this centre is to practise visualization techniques. As we see colours and shapes more clearly, it indicates to us that part of our third eye is awakening.

If part of our third eye has been opened through shock or psychic practices we may have power without the wisdom which a gentle progressive opening of the third eye would bestow.

When I was first exploring the esoteric world of hidden forces I met a woman who was a spaced out psychic. She often had clairvoyant pictures of people's futures, precognitive flashes and a whole range of psychic experiences.

She worked briefly as a hypnotherapist and she could see the pictures that were in her client's mind. On one occasion she decided to experiment. During a visualization she took her client through a meadow bordered by a hedge. As he walked through his meadow she sent a beam out from her third eye and placed into his picture a bright pink stile in the hedge. Then she said casually, 'Soon you will be reaching the end of the pathway. Look around and tell me what you can see.' Her client jumped in surprise and exclaimed that there was a bright pink stile in the hedge! This was pretty harmless but I am sure many of us have part of our third eye open and place things in people's minds without being consciously aware of it. As we become more evolved it behoves us to watch our thoughtforms. They are very powerful and can be used to create havoc or healing.

When we have the choice of placing love or fear directly into people's minds we have a tremendous responsibility to humankind.

In the etheric of our third eye is held the blueprint of our past lives. Naturally when this chakra is open we are able to access the information we need.

Those who are attracted to read this book will have had past lives of wisdom, of healing, of esoteric knowledge. We have gifts, potential and strengths at a soul level which can become available to us.

Dedicating ourselves

I believe that as we put out the intention to raise our vibrations, as we dedicate ourselves to the service of humankind and to the Universe, as we meditate and focus on the Light, so our third eye becomes clear and bright. We transmit a higher frequency and our light draws more evolved guides to us who want to work with us. This is an honour and a responsibility.

If we respond to the guidance of these greater guides who approach us, we can together accomplish wonderful things and help many souls.

There are many highly evolved guides in spirit now who are drawn to work with those on the Earth Plane in its time of transition. They are looking for people of sufficient dedication and integrity to work with.

This does not necessarily mean sitting channelling all day. It does mean being dedicated to Truth, Integrity and Service and to listening to the promptings of spirit so that we allow ourselves to be used.

We are called on now to do spiritual work amongst the

rush and bustle of people. We can no longer withdraw to quiet spiritual sanctuaries to work. The tests are harder now for those devoting themselves to Service. Of course, the rewards at a soul level are greater too. Many who have had a difficult but dedicated life are going to be delighted when they pass over and see what they have accomplished. It is worth it.

The path of bliss

When our third eye is awake we feel joy. In the lower centres we are open to happiness. Joy is of a higher spiritual quality.

Over a period of time I have asked for a number of lessons. Each time I asked for a lesson I was well and truly tested. I have often felt submerged or bombarded by the tests thrown up by these lessons. One day I decided that I had better walk the Path of Bliss! How naive!

When we walk the Path of Bliss we are living at a third eye level. It is the Path which bridges heaven and earth.

The more I contemplated the Path of Bliss the more I realized that it was no easy option. I realized that in order to walk in bliss I would have to let go of my attachment to everything. Every time I chose to feel anger instead of bliss I would be stepping off my pathway. So I would even have to give up my attachment to anger!

At one time the Path of Bliss was simply the path of non-attachment. Now, as in all matters spiritual, more is expected of those who aspire to walk this high Path. It is only possible when our heart centre and higher chakras are open.

When we wallow in self-pity, hurt, blame or in the

past, we are walking in the mud. It is selfishness. It is a lower Path.

The Path of Bliss is a dry Path. We are expected to switch our consciousness to a higher level whenever we encounter muddy emotions. On the high Path we meet with all conditions. The wind, rain and snow buffet us because we are more exposed, not less so. The sun bakes us. And we must walk through these conditions and not be affected by them.

If people throw stones at us on this Path we must never retaliate. We must smile and move on and not allow those of lower understanding to deflect us, for the Path of Bliss is a Path of harmlessness.

When it is raining and we say, 'It's a bad day,' we are on a lower Path. Our unconscious mind, which is our computer, does not know we are talking of the weather. It thinks we wish to create a bad day! If we repeat this instruction often enough we attract a bad day to ourself. That is the Law of Cause and Effect, karma.

On the Path of Bliss we are above karma. We are on a Path of Love and love transmutes karma.

There are rewards for those who walk the Path of Bliss. Our eyes are more open to beauty. Our ears attuned to celestial sounds and to the transmissions from Source. We cannot walk along this Path unless we are prepared to listen to the Divine voice and trust it to guide us, for it is a narrow Path and easy to step off.

However when we rise to the rainbow arc between Heaven and Earth we will bring forward the new higher Truths which are being disseminated to the Earth Plane. These are the seeds of the new higher teachings, so as we scatter them we are sowing sacred seeds, some of which will fall on fertile ground and grow.

When we walk the Path of Bliss steadfastly holding our vision and intention we are world servers and are beacons of light to fortify others. The greatest reward for walking the Path of Bliss is inner peace.

CHAPTER 19

Towards Enlightenment

At the crown centre we link with God or Source. This chakra is symbolized by the thousand petalled lotus, the flower with a thousand petals, which sits at the very top of our head. Each petal represents a doorway which we must open within ourselves on our journey to enlightenment.

We can only open up our crown chakra petal-by-petal through meditation and spiritual practices. When every petal is open and each doorway to self realization is explored, we are truly enlightened. We then no longer have to incarnate on Earth.

So the thousand petalled lotus symbolizes our journey to enlightenment. Its roots are founded in the mud of ignorance, which is our base chakra. From here it commits itself to growth through the water of emotion and awakening until it reaches the Light, the crown chakra, where it can open fully.

Physical images of the crown chakra

The halo commonly seen around the heads of holy people in old paintings indicates the crown centre being open. Men of high standing used to wear tall hats to emphasize their nearness to God. A cloth cap suggested that workers were lower down the spiritual ladder! Royalty wear crowns to symbolize their allegiance to God while the hierarchy of the Church wear tall headgear for the same reason. Many monks shave the crown of their heads to signify their submission to God. Native American Indian chiefs wear full headdresses. Each feather symbolizes a petal of the crown chakra open.

Each time we pass an initiation test in a lifetime and earn a colour, that colour radiates from our crown centre, like the feathers of an Indian headdress. Once earned we have that quality forever. These colours may be, for instance, a whole spectrum of greens for working with and for nature, healing with plants or herbal medicine. We may have had lifetimes of total dedication to study, which will have earned us a few shades of yellow. Lifetimes of loving heart centred service may have earned us a few pink feathers. There will be some with gold, earned by acquiring wisdom. These permanent colours in our crown centre are not necessarily the same as the mental and emotional colours we are radiating in our aura.

Blessings and grace are offered to us through our crown centre, by touching our head.

In many communities it is considered an insult to touch someone on the top of the head. This affirms how very sensitive this centre is – a sensitive person can be knocked off balance if hit here.

Our hair is recognized as our crowning glory. Metaphysically, hair represents our strength because it is created by our thoughts. If we have neat, straight hair we are likely to have clear, simple thinking patterns. If our hair is untidy and wild our thoughts are certainly more muddled. The person with long, shiny hair has more healthy thoughts than the person with lank, straggly hair. People who tense up their scalps so that the hair follicle receives too little nourishment to live become bald. They have tense thoughts.

Choosing to open or close

Our thoughts create our lives. They shape the decisions which decide our destiny. They open or close our doors to enlightenment.

When our crown chakra is closed and dormant we are spiritually asleep. Non-enlightenment is a prison. All we see is the four walls of our cell and miss everything going on beyond. Such a person will be totally unaware of psychic and spiritual whispers and will live in a world where the only reality is what he can see, hear and touch with his physical senses.

There have been many souls in incarnation who have been living behind locked doors but that is changing rapidly. Spiritual doors in the minds of man are flying open with great rapidity. It is as if an amnesty has been declared and hordes of prisoners are being let out of prison. They are confused and frightened. It is up to those of higher vision and integrity to soothe them and lead them across the bridge to higher awareness.

The crown chakra is the centre of knowing. When this centre is open, we do not see or hear or sense, we simply *know*. It does not matter what anyone else says, we have an inner knowing.

Opening this centre brings illumination, enlightenment and liberation from the restrictions of non-belief and lesser awareness. It brings a new perspective about the meaning of the Universe.

When this centre is fully open we *know* we are one with God. We are not part of all that is. We *are* all that is. Here we know we are one with everyone. There is no separation. All just is. The colour of this chakra is violet white, a delicate and light vibration.

No one can help us to open our crown centre. This has to be the result of our own inner journeying and exploration. However here is a series of yoga-based exercises designed to open each chakra in turn. They are exercises which I have found helpful.

OPENING THE CHAKRAS

No chakra should be opened in isolation, so doing these regularly, with concentration and awareness, is one way of opening doors. In order to maximize the positive benefits of each exercise we must focus on the chakra we are working on (refer back to the diagram on page 93). If we relax, the results will be much deeper and swifter. Affirmations will slip into our consciousness more readily.

Before starting the session lie for a few minutes on the floor, straight but relaxed. Breathe comfortably.

Base Centre
- Kneel, sitting back on your heels.
- Rub the base of your spine for a few moments.

- Breathe rhythmically into your base centre until you sense it becoming red and warm.
- Place your hands on your knees.
- As you exhale, tighten up your perineum and flex your spine in the pelvic area so that your back is convex.
- As you inhale, flex your pelvis forward so that your back is concave.
- Repeat this several times.
- Relax, breathing comfortably into the base centre for a minute.
- Affirmation – *I am safe, secure and grounded.*

Sacral Centre

- Kneel, sitting back on your heels and gently rub your abdomen and spine at the sacral centre for a few moments.
- Breathe rhythmically into your sacral centre until you sense it becoming orange and warm.
- Move on to all fours with your back straight.
- As you exhale hump your spine up and tighten your abdomen, flexing your spine with head and bottom down.
- As you inhale lift your head and buttocks and make your back concave.
- Repeat several times focusing on the sacral centre.
- Relax, breathing comfortably into the sacral centre for a minute.
- Affirmation – *I master my emotions.*
  I lovingly give and receive.

Solar Plexus Centre

- Sit with your legs crossed and back straight.
- Gently rub your solar plexus and the spine at the back of your solar plexus for a few moments.

- Breathe rhythmically into your solar plexus until you sense it growing golden yellow and warm.
- Raise your elbows and hold your shoulders with your hands, fingers at the front and thumbs at the back.
- Exhale and hold your breath as you twist to the left. Count to four. Re-centre and inhale.
- Hold your breath as you twist to the right. Count to 4. Re-centre, exhale.
- Repeat several times. Pause for a few moments, then reverse directions.
- Relax, breathing comfortably into the solar plexus for a minute.
- Affirmation – *I am confident.*
  I claim my power.

Heart Centre

- Sit with your legs crossed and back straight.
- Gently rub your chest and the spine at the back of your heart centre.
- Breathe rhythmically into your heart centre until you sense it becoming green and warm.
- Extend your legs in front of you.
- Bend your right leg and place your right foot on the outside of your left knee.
- Hold your right knee with your hands and bring your chin down to your knee.
- Breathe in as you lift your spine and head.
- Breathe out as you swing your right arm back taking your body round as far as it will go. Look round over your right shoulder. Hold for several moments.
- Breathe in as you bring your arm back.
- Breathe out as you bring your chin down to your knee again.

- Repeat three times. Then repeat on the other side.
- Relax, breathing comfortably into your heart centre, for a minute.
- Affirmation — *I openly give and receive love.*

Throat Centre

- Sit with your legs crossed and back straight.
- Gently rub your throat and the back of your neck for a few moments.
- Breathe rhythmically into your throat centre until you sense it growing turquoise and warm.
- Grasp your knees and keep your arms straight.
- Breathe out as you flex your upper spine and bring your chin down into your throat.
- Breathe in as you flex your upper spine and lean your head back.
- Repeat several times. Rest for a few moments.
- Breathe out as you shrug your shoulders up.
- Breathe in as you bring your shoulders down.
- Repeat several times.
- Breathe out and shrug shoulders up. Hold for the count of 15.
- Relax, breathing comfortably into your throat centre, for a minute.
- Affirmation — *I speak my truth.*
              I communicate honestly.

Third Eye

- Sit with your legs crossed and back straight.
- Gently massage round hairline, eyes, ears and then rub forehead and back of head behind the third eye.
- Breathe rhythmically into your third eye until you sense it becoming indigo and warm.

185

- Lock your fingertips just in front of your throat.
- Breathe in and hold.
- Squeeze your abdomen and sphincter muscles and squeeze the energy up as if you are squeezing a ball up your body.
- Breathe out and raise your arm above your head with your fingers still gripping as you push the ball out of the top of your head.
- Repeat twice.
- Relax, breathing comfortably into your third eye, for a minute.
- Affirmation – *God and I are one.*

Crown Chakra

- Stand straight with your feet slightly apart.
- Breathe rhythmically into your crown centre as you imagine the petals opening.
- Raise your hands above your head to reach to the Highest.
- Bend from the base centre until your hands touch the ground and the energy is focused at the crown of your head.
- Breathe comfortably.
- Raise your torso slowly.
- Relax, breathing comfortably into your crown centre for a minute.
- Affirmation – *I submit to the Divine.*

If you find it difficult to kneel or sit cross legged, these exercises may be done sitting on a chair.

Opening our chakras is our journey to enlightenment and peace within.

CHAPTER 20

The Higher Purpose

There is always a spiritual reason behind everything that happens on the Earth Plane. Nothing happens senselessly. There is always a higher purpose.

We see things from such a limited perspective. To an ant a dog may be an impenetrable forest of hair which vibrates when he thunders, while to a cat he may be a large four-legged enemy, who barks and sleeps in the house at night. A bird flying above the house may see the dog as a furry creature who chases cats, goes for walks with humans and is owned by them, while the owner perceives him as an intelligent, faithful companion who shares his life.

Only Source knows the whole interconnecting pattern of the dog's relationships, its evolution and growth, its purpose on Earth and how its life fits into the vast Plan. Suppose the dog was shot by its cruel guard in another life. At some time the dog comes back to repay the karma. In the country where the guard re-incarnates, perhaps as a young woman, certain dogs are being bred with vicious qualities. On a higher plane it is decided that this must be curbed. The only way to draw people's attention to these dangerous dogs is for a number of attacks to take place at the same time. So the dog returns in the body of one of these dangerous dogs and attacks the young woman who shot it in an earlier life. Because of public concern about these attacks that strain of dog is no longer bred. The spiritual jigsaw is complete.

The seemingly terrible things that happen on Earth always serve our growth or the expansion of the planet in some way.

The challenge of violence

Tibet was an advanced spiritual society. A group of highly evolved souls incarnated there again and again and the Light became stronger and brighter. Much wisdom and esoteric knowledge was focused in one small part of the planet. It was time for this ancient wisdom to be spread around the globe. The Chinese invasion of Tibet was and is a horrendous violation. At a higher level, it forced the Dalai Llama and many of his monks to flee. In their quest for world support for Tibet they are carrying the Light around the whole world.

No one can demonstrate peace and non-violence unless they have an aggressor to be tested by! Gandhi and thousands of great souls with him who knew these truths stood up and showed the world the power of non-aggression. They were mighty spiritual warriors.

When I was in an ashram in India I copied down these words about non-violence which, as a person with much to learn about anger, really touched me at my core.

'Non-violence. There is no response equal to

non-violence. There is no vow equal to speaking Truth. There is no discipline greater than control of mind.

'Non-violence is an alternate name of Truth and Love. By following non-violence one achieves love. Non-violence is a resplendent and lofty ideal. To follow the path of non-violence it is necessary to change the mental attitude.

'Only those who are ready to sacrifice their desires would be able to follow the path of non-violence. Nobody should be harmed by mind, speech or body – not even think of it. By purity of thought, word and deed one should serve even one's enemies. Overwhelm the bad and jealous by your goodness. Humility is the main character of those who wish to don the mantle of non-violence. The coward and the immoral cannot achieve non-violence, and by means of peace, love and truth, one should attain non-violence.'

Tests along the way

No one climbs Mount Everest without training and we certainly do not send a child up such a challenging mountain. No one becomes a Light worker without going through many tests and challenges. It is out of seeming disasters that strong souls emerge. A young soul is not even offered these opportunities for growth.

No one would expect to make a five-year-old the Managing Director of a company. A good M.D. has been tried, tested and proved. He has had to take difficult decisions, deal with problems, overcome crises and keep his head and his confidence throughout. Then he is considered worthy of the task.

So when we wish to have spiritual promotion we sign on at a higher level to a course where we know we will be tried and tested. We may be presented with difficult decisions, have complicated problems to overcome or be faced with a crisis or shock or two. Other people will offer themselves in service to us to allow us to have our testing experience.

That awkward, intransigent man in the office may at a higher level be a close spiritual friend offering to help us to learn a lesson. The person who rams his car into ours when we are driving sedately along may have volunteered to teach us the particular lesson we need for our spiritual promotion. The person who comes into our life and tempts us just when we are vulnerable is testing our integrity.

So the less time we spend complaining about our lot, the more energy we will have to do something about the situation – to face the test, and move on.

The other side of tragedy

There is always a higher purpose behind seemingly motiveless deaths. A man is stabbed to death by someone who is an acknowledged danger to the public and the law is changed. Children die at a recognized black spot on the road and the road is widened. People die in a boating accident because of lax rules and the regulations are tightened up.

However spiritually aware their loved ones are, they still go through the emotional pain that such deaths cause and it is an important part of the healing process for them to acknowledge the numbness, grief, rage and intense pain. It sometimes helps, however, to know that they died to save many other souls. It was not by chance. When public attention needs to be drawn to an unsatisfactory situation a horrific happening galvanizes people into action. In most cases the people who die have offered themselves in this service. They have completed their chosen life span, however short, and have to choose a way of passing over. Their death is also an act of service.

Occasionally there are cases of injustice so glaring that campaigns are started to redress the harm done. It often seems that we need to be presented with something totally outrageous before we take the steps needed. Whenever we need a spiritual kick to get us moving at a higher level someone offers to be the 'victim'. However it will fit in with his karma too and will always serve his growth.

If a child is damaged by hospital neglect, the parents are presented with a challenge. Only they can know the lesson offered. It may be to gather their courage to sue the hospital in order to get money to help their damaged child. It may be to campaign to expose a situation of public neglect. It may be to accept what has happened with forgiveness. They must meditate on the lesson and act accordingly. However nothing can be done to us unless at a soul level we have agreed to it. So the child will also have lessons to learn or a service to offer.

If faced with clarity and courage, these tests that at a higher level we have chosen to experience will strengthen us and offer us lessons.

Listening to our intuition

Because Planet Earth is now moving to a higher level, when new karma is about to be created very often someone will step in and intervene to prevent it. However, if karma is being repaid or someone is offering themselves in service to humankind, others do not feel inspired to prevent it in any way. We all have an inner knowing about these matters. Many of the horrendous happenings we see now are a just repayment of karmic debt.

Sandra was attacked with an iron bar by a mentally ill person she had tried to befriend. She defended herself as well as she could with her bare hands against this woman but she was repeatedly clubbed by the frenzied woman and was getting weak from pain. As she was about to lose consciousness there was a small diversion which distracted her attacker.

In that moment Sandra left her body and was met by her father in spirit who told her that she must fight for her life. In previous lives she had given up. This time her lesson was to stand up for herself.

Instantly she was back in her body with the strength to try just once more to repel the attacker long enough for help to arrive.

Sandra was desperately badly injured. She recovered eventually, though she was still damaged.

This savage attack taught her to listen to her intuition at all times. She had not wanted to meet the woman that day but had overriden her guiding voice. She realized that life was precious and she was spending too much time doing heavy things she did not want to do. She left her job and started to do what she really felt alive and happy doing.

She started to live. At the same time the experience set her on a seek-and-search into the meaning of life and the Laws of the Universe.

Hannah had been living for ten years in a very happy, loving relationship. She felt her husband was her soul mate and that they would be together for the whole of this life in a mutually supportive, close relationship. One morning she woke feeling a terrible sense of premonition. She got out of bed and was sick. She struggled to work and fainted but managed to get through the day.

That evening her husband was going to a meeting. She waved goodbye to him, thinking, 'Something's going to happen tonight. It will never be the same again.'

At that meeting he met and fell in love with a young woman. Hannah was devastated. Her husband moved in almost immediately with the young woman but kept coming back to see her. She felt sure his relationship with the girl would not last, but another part of her was full of hurt and grief and fear that he would not come back.

Yet another part of her wanted to learn the higher lessons. 'Why should my Higher Self have allowed this to happen to me?' she cried. She began a seek-and-search for the past-life implications of what had happened. Many pieces of the jigsaw of her life fell into place and she felt happier. She understood that she and this other woman had been rivals over this man many times in other lives. In the past she had always hung on, been totally dependent, and had fallen to pieces when she lost him. She knew that this time she must detach herself from the need to have him.

She started to work on herself. As she took away the layers of her fears, she revealed to herself that she had gifts and talents that were not being used. She found a new job which expanded and fulfilled her.

Hannah started to do many things alone and became more confident and secure in herself. At the same time she recognized that she was hurt and full of grief for her loss and became gentler with herself and others.

Every day she visualized herself snipping away her dependency cords with her partner and prayed for the perfect partner to come in for her. Although she secretly hoped it would be this same man whom she loved, she never let him enter her visualization and was prepared to let him go. She then blessed him and asked for the highest good to come to him.

Within a few months, he realized how empty his new relationship was and how foolish he had been. She took him back but she was wiser now, less dependent and needy. She knew that out of that hurt and pain, a much stronger Hannah had emerged. She told me that excruciating though the experience had been, she knew that the other woman had totally served her growth.

Gentle souls

There are many mighty, evolved souls amongst us. Take a soul who has grown to a point of gentle peace and non-aggression. Can you imagine the tests such a soul would undergo if he offered to be born into a violent family in order to bring peace into their midst?

I knew a child once, Michael, who radiated such an aura of calm. His brother was insecure, jealous, angry and quarrelsome but when Michael was around all was calm. He stayed with our family when his parents were away. It was at a time when things were pretty fraught in our lives and there was a lot of arguing going on. During the entire time of his stay there was not one cross word.

I was friendly with a woman called Laura. She was born into a family where there was a lot of friction. Her father was angry, her mother was insecure, her brother and sisters quarrelsome. She told me that she always knew it was nothing to do with her. They would talk about getting their own back, about getting one over someone. They constantly discussed material things. Even as a small child she used to think, 'That's not what life is about.' She never argued. Nor did she collude with their ignorance. She just accepted them and sent out her thoughts of Truth. Later, in adulthood, she learnt that she was a volunteer, one who came to Earth without karma to help others.

From power struggles to cooperation

In a spiritually evolved society the government acts as a wise parent. Those elected to government make sensible laws and encourage and inspire their people. They protect the needy and work for the highest good. Where the state does not protect the vulnerable members or acts unfairly or ruthlessly, then factions of people will rebel or find some other way of expressing their disaffection with the leaders. The Government acting without integrity reflects the disintegration within the mass of people. This is a state of mind and emotion we are seeing in many countries now.

I was at a meeting once where there were about thirty adults. Everyone had differing views to express. People were clinging to their individual pet ideas. Most of the participants had an investment in doing things their own way or getting something out of the situation. The atmosphere was tense and uptight. The children reflected the fragmented atmosphere, behaving disruptively and very noisily.

Finally I suggested that we link together and attune, then, letting go of what we wanted from the situation, take time to meditate on what we could offer for the highest good of all. Everyone agreed and we had a short meditation.

The effect was instantaneous and almost unbelievable. The children, who mirrored the adults' feelings, became as good as gold. The younger ones quietly drew pictures. The older ones felt safe enough to go out and play. The adults started constructively suggesting what they could offer to help. The emphasis shifted from need and power struggle to sharing and giving.

When families, schools, communities, countries stop demanding for their needs to be met and instead attune together to decide on what they can offer for the highest good of all, young unevolved souls will feel safe and older souls will work together in service.

Then peace spreads like a soothing balm from families to communities to countries and to the planet as a whole. With peace comes the power to act wisely.

CHAPTER 21

Healing Energy

As the vibrations of the planet rise, more and more people are feeling the pull towards the Light. When we sense this our chakras start to open and we begin to feel a desire to heal ourselves and others.

When we open our heart centre and truly love another, whether we are laying on hands or sending them loving thoughts, a healing must take place at some level.

That healing energy goes to their soul, for the wisdom of the soul to use appropriately. A shift may take place in attitude. A feeling of anger may diminish. A grief may lessen or dissolve. A healing may manifest in the physical body.

We can be certain that when we enfold another with love everyone in the Universe is affected, for every thought has a chain reaction.

Blocks to healing

In the Aquarian Age it is no longer enough to attune to the Highest and hold the client in the Light while channelling healing energy to them. We are asked to raise our energies consistently to a higher vibration. We cannot do this while smoking, drinking or behaving compulsively in order to bury our own emotions and fears.

We are now asked to take responsibility for ourselves and heal our own blocks. As we do so, we automatically heal others – nothing happens in isolation. When we heal our own blocks others are touched by our knowing and they too make shifts in consciousness. No one can come to a change in awareness without a healing taking place at an emotional or physical level.

People often say to me that they really want to heal others and feel they could do it but are not sure if they are good enough. When someone is interested in healing and has a burning desire to do it, then they are ready. Some people are naturals at it. Others need some guidance.

The intention we have when we heal is most important. If we get a sense of importance from giving healing, we are using ego and this can prevent healing from taking place as our ego keeps us separate. Healing is oneness. We offer ourselves as a channel. If we think, 'Please let this work. I do hope it works,' we are thinking of self, which means we are separate from the person we are healing. So one principle of healing is that we must be quite detached from the results and be accepting if no healing appears to take place or if the recipient feels nothing. We can do no more than raise our consciousness and offer ourselves.

If the client is not willing to be healed then there is nothing we can do. After all a client may have a pay-off from his illness. It may be the only time he gets attention. It may prevent him from doing a job he dislikes. Being sick may be the only time he can justify having a rest. No doubt on a conscious level he will want to be healed, but unconsciously he may not be ready to let go.

This reminds me of the story of the person who said, 'Please only make me a little bit better, just well enough to be comfortable but still get my invalidity pension.' I always thought it was an apocryphal story until I heard it myself! It is by no means unusual for people to want to heal the symptoms without being ready to take responsibility for the cause.

When we channel healing to someone, we have to trust their Higher Self to use the energy in the most appropriate way. The person may not learn the lesson offered by the illness if a physical healing takes place, so their Higher Self may choose to use the energy at a different level.

When we channel healing energy with pure intention a healing must take place at some level.

Opening up to energy

Unless all our chakras are open, we may not be channelling the healing rays the client needs. One healer may be wonderful at lifting headaches, while another can release cancer. Soul to soul the sick person may have made a contract to allow someone else to heal them instead of us. It really is not for us to judge. We merely offer our services and let go. However, the vast majority of people do respond to healing.

In order to be able to heal we must be able to open our chakras. We can, of course, do this with visualization. However, when our intentions are pure and we feel true compassion, our chakras will open automatically. They will open to the extent that we can raise our vibrations.

So the higher we can raise our vibrations, the higher we can raise the consciousness of the person we are working with, and the higher the level of divine energy we bring through.

Healing energy flows through us like a current of electricity. If we bring down a very high voltage charge into our crown centre, we transform it through our chakras to the level the client can take. When properly attuned, we trust the wisdom of our Higher Self to do this for us.

As with all things, we must apply common sense. If we find we are capable of bringing down a high charge of healing energy but we have a blockage in our heart centre, we can damage ourself. We will know because we will feel dizzy or our heart will start beating fast. We are being told to slow down, take care and do some more personal growth work to clear out blockages.

Grounding and cleansing

Healing energy is no earthly use to us or the person we are serving if we cannot ground it. One of the best exercises for grounding is walking, but most exercise tends to ground us. Putting our feet flat on the floor, sensing roots going down into the earth and firmly linking us to the earth is also a good way. If we are sitting cross legged, we can picture a grounding cord going down into the earth from the base of our spine.

The person we are healing also needs to be grounded. This can be done by asking them to put their feet firmly on the ground or by visualizing roots going down. Putting our hands on their feet will also ground them.

If we are sensitive and open our chakras will pick up all sorts of impure feelings and thoughts from the atmosphere and the people around us. When we are healing others we are wide open to their energy. They may be mentally ill or have some really nasty thought forms around them that are causing their emotional or physical problems. We will automatically take all that dark energy into our chakras.

As long as our chakras are working properly, we will be able to transform that heavy energy and return it clear and clean to the cosmos. However, if we have blockages or are not in perfect condition ourselves, we will become very drained, depleted or irritable. When a healer becomes irritable, blaming or depressed it is a sure sign that they are taking in others' negativity and are not cleansing themselves properly.

If a sea anemone is in a polluted pool where it can only take in polluted energy, it is going to find it very difficult to stay pure and clean. Healers are no different. We need to get away from dark situations, have rest time, relaxation and fun.

Walking in nature is a very good way of cleansing our chakras. Deep breathing in an unpolluted atmosphere is another. Swimming, showering, bathing are all ways of purifying ourselves. As always if we cannot do these things, we can visualize ourselves walking in nature, picture ourselves swimming or showering. This helps to wash the impurities from our chakras. Listening to beautiful music or to a tape of nature's sounds, especially running water, can help to cleanse and purify us. Physically cleaning our living space is a cleansing ceremony.

Many of us are very inclined to look at all our negative traits. We look at the mirrors of bad people, situations and emotions we have drawn into our lives.

When I give talks I occasionally remind people that they have also attracted in the positive and beautiful people, situations and emotions that are in their lives. I ask them to think of some of these good things. Then I remind them that they could not perceive or be aware of these good qualities if they did not also have them.

If I ask them to relate these good qualities they possess to the person next to them, the atmosphere becomes warm. The first time I asked people to do this exercise in a hall full of people, they were all taking their sweaters off by the time they had finished. Their heart chakras were expanding and becoming warm.

When we attune to our Higher Self and to the Higher Self of the person we are healing, then link both to Source or God, we are totally guided.

Whenever we raise our consciousness with the intention of helping someone, Higher Beings see our Light and respond.

Letting go

During the first healing class I ever ran we went through the basics of grounding, attuning, raising energies, setting pure intentions and linking to Source through our Higher Selves. We raised a very high energy in the room.

One of the young men had never given healing before but he felt strongly guided to leave his hands a few inches from his partner's body at the heart centre. She could feel the stream of healing energy pouring into her chest. At the same time she could physically feel hands on her stomach. When she opened her eyes to check, of course, there were no human hands there. A Higher Being was taking the opportunity offered by the raised vibrations to come in and help with the healing.

This now happens so often during healing classes that I advise participants beforehand so that they are not surprised by the sensation of invisible spirit hands working on their body.

When we give someone healing we open ourselves up. We also open up the other person. So it is important to close ourself and them down before we send them out into the world again. A complete protection would be to visualize each of the chakras closing like a flower and then sealing each one with a cross in a circle, which is an ancient symbol of protection. If we then surround the person with a cocoon of light, the healing energy can continue to work safely within them. Of course, they will automatically open up when they are ready.

It is also important for the healer to uncord herself from the client or they may continue to draw energy from her whenever they think of her. We can do this by imagining ourselves snipping the cords away, or by visualizing a waterfall washing us clean or by physically washing our hands.

Of course, if as a healer we are totally free of blocks, pure in thought, have opened all our chakras and can raise our consciousness to Source, we will not need to do any of these things for we will be a pure channel!

Using oil and sound

I once read a story about a group who was giving healing to a girl. The girl did not feel anything and yet the healers could all sense the healing energy flowing through them. A clairvoyant came into the room and could see the cloud of healing energy floating above the girl but unable to enter her body. He gently rubbed some oil onto her forehead, whereupon the healing energy spiralled into her body where she could instantly feel its effect.

I was reminded of this story when I was running an Enlightenment week where we were raising our consciousness to very high levels. Before our evening session one of the course participants had given me an aromatherapy massage and my back especially felt relaxed and glowing. During the attunement at the start of the session I could feel my back getting hotter and hotter until it felt on fire. There was a gasp from the other side of the circle for they could all see an intense golden light surrounding me and entering my body, then spreading round the circle in both directions. It felt as if the oil was the medium by which this amazing energy entered my physical body and it remained with me through the night.

Since that experience I often suggest the use of a little oil rubbed in when people are giving healing.

The physical problems in our body are caused by blocked energy. This is a condensed, heavy, negative vibration. In advanced civilizations sound was used to break up these blockages so that life force could flow again. Medical science uses ultra sound, which shakes up and loosens the negative vibrations.

It is cheaper and more effective to tune into the note of the blockage and find the sound vibration to start shaking it up. In our healing groups we often give healing by letting the perfect sound vibrate through the person who is receiving healing. They invariably report feeling cleaned out and amazing. Often they say they feel as if they were vibrating from head to toe.

The choice to heal

When we give someone healing we lift their consciousness to God. In the mind of God we are all whole and perfect, so when we raise someone to this level of consciousness miracles are possible.

When I think of the word inspiration I imagine a church full of prayer and goodwill. The spire of the church lifts all that prayer and goodwill to God. So when we inspire someone, we lift them to God. All things are then possible.

Inspiration means to breathe life into someone. Every word we utter has an effect. We must ask ourselves. 'Do our words give life force or take it away? Do we heal others or kill? Do we light them up or damp their flame down?'

A client complained to me about her unemployed daughter. She told me she wanted to help her and in the same breath said, 'She sits eating ice cream all day. She's a big, fat, lazy slob.' Then she added hastily that she never said that to her face of course. I reminded her that her daughter was picking up her thoughts as effectively as if she was saying the words and was responding to them. The mother was an extremely powerful lady with strong, angry thoughts which battered the girl's aura.

I persuaded her to find a photo of her daughter when she was slim, happy and in work. I asked her to focus on that picture and keep remembering times when she had been happy and flowing and alive. She promised to keep projecting out that positive picture of her daughter.

Two weeks later she told me that the result was almost

unbelievable. 'Within a couple of days, without me saying a word, my daughter put herself on a diet and stuck to it. She looks so much better and happier already.'

Now it is absolutely true that if the daughter had a whole unbroken aura, her mother's thoughts could not penetrate it and affect her. However very few of us are that complete. So our thoughts can help to heal others or destroy them.

I was talking to a meditation teacher. She was a delightful person, very tuned into healing. She constantly dedicated candles to healing people and places. Whenever she watched the news she sent love and light to anyone in need. I gave her my first book, *Light Up Your Life*. She phoned me up and said that as she read it she realized she was sending healing to just about everyone in the world except her son. She worried about him. He was unemployed, a heavy smoker and living in a squat. After she read *Light Up Your Life* she consistently focused loving, healing thoughts on him. She lit candles for him. Within a week he phoned out of the blue and said, 'Guess what, Mum? I've given up smoking and I'm looking for a job.'

When we so love others that we transcend our little personality selves healing takes place. When we heal others a mantle of peace enfolds us.

CHAPTER 22

Miracles and Synchronicity

Miracles, synchronicities and coincidences are all automatic responses to the correct use of the Spiritual Laws of the Universe. More and more people are seeking spiritual healing and alternative therapies, or natural therapies as I prefer to call them. Cures and transformations are often reported even in cases which defy medical expertise. It is not surprising. The body responds to a re-alignment of its natural energies. The psyche responds to truly loving care and empathy. So miracles are inevitable. And cures which take place over time are still miracles. They are miracles slowed down.

Mere mortals would find it impossible to be in the right place at the right time without unseen forces guiding them. It would be like an orchestra trying to play without a conductor. Our spirit guides synchronize our timings so that we are where we are supposed to be. They guide lovers destined to meet to adjacent seats on the same aeroplane when the moment is right. They guide the patient who is ready to the perfect healer. There is no chance. When we meet someone, our Spirit Guides have organized it for us. When the same things happen at the same time all over the world, Higher Forces are oiling the wheels of synchronicity.

Coincidences happen all the time. We discover that everyone in the room has the same birth sign. We realize that all the men in our life had a mother called June. This makes us think and wonder.

We already know

I always leave a pad and pen by my bed to jot down thoughts or dreams which come to me during the night. One morning I looked at my scrawl across the page. It said, 'When you ask a question you already know the answer.'

I wondered about this for some time before I realized that this was really true. At some level we know all things. *When we are ready to formulate the question, then we are ready to reveal the answer to ourself.* This means we will recognize the answer when it is presented to us. It may come in a newspaper article or we may hear someone say what we need to hear and we will register it. It may be shown to us in some symbolic form which we will translate as the solution to our question. When we trust this more and more we are ready to move forward.

One day I was lying in the bath and a voice said to me, 'Go to India.' I had for some years been interested in the avatar Sai Baba's teachings and he had occasionally appeared in my dreams and meditations. I knew at once that I was being told to go to India to Sai Baba's ashram and I immediately jumped out of the bath to look at my diary to see when I was free to go. With a little juggling I cleared out two weeks the following February.

Then I started to think, 'How will I find out where to go and what to do?' Next morning I had a new client. I knew nothing about her and she started to talk about her problems. Suddenly she stopped in mid-flow and said, 'Do you know Sai Baba?' I replied that I was intending to go to his ashram in February. It transpired that she was a devotee of his, knew all the people and information I needed and was tremendously helpful to me in organizing my trip.

On my last day in India I had a delightful experience. I popped into a craft emporium. My eye was immediately caught by an enormous batik of a white elephant, its trunk upraised, bearing a king and queen on its back. The effect was spectacular and I gazed at it in wonder. I left the shop to buy some more presents but kept remembering that elephant batik. Back I went to have another look. As I examined it again a tiny, thin, elderly Indian lady touched me on the arm. 'You like it?' she asked. 'I think it's magnificent.' Her face was wreathed in smiles and it transpired she was the artist. She showed me her other works and explained the spiritual significance behind each one. Then we went to have a cup of char together while I decided whether or not to buy it.

We sat companionably by the side of a busy road drinking char and she told me how she had started her spiritual quest. One day she was feeling particularly depressed about the violence in India and the state of the planet. She felt burdened, frightened of the power of those in government and helpless to do anything to change the situation. It was in this dark despairing, helpless state that she fell asleep one afternoon.

A Being of Light came to her and took her on a journey to look down on Planet Earth. She saw the magnificent translucent colours of the Earth, like a wonderful pearl nestling in a blue sea. Then she was taken to see the dark, ugly scars of humankind's legacy to the planet. She was shown how these pockets of blackness were absorbed into the Earth, how they marked the surface of the planet and affected the aura around it. Lastly she was taken out into the Universe to see its vastness and magnificence.

When she returned from her spiritual journey, she felt very shaken. She was frail and elderly and did not feel she had the courage to speak out against the bad people of the world, so she used her art to spread a message of peace.

The little old Indian lady's face glowed as she talked and I gasped as I heard her story for it was so uncannily similar to the spiritual journey I was taken on, which set me on my spiritual pathway!

I describe this journey in my second book, *A Time for Transformation*. Briefly, at a time when I was in suicidal despair, a golden Being came to me and took me on a journey through the Planes of the Universe and told me I was to teach. That hour changed the course of my life. I now shared my story with my elderly companion. Since I had my original experience many people have said to me, 'Why you?' Some have added, 'Why you of all people who had no spiritual beliefs?'

What I had had throughout my life was a willingness to do good, a desire to serve, so I must have had a light. And at that moment of blackness, the cry for help went out from the depth of my soul and activated a response from the Universal energy.

Some years after my life-changing experience, as I sat in meditation, I asked why I had been given that experience. I was told that everyone is given such an opportunity at some time. For some it comes as a dream, for others as a vision but most people doubt their dreams and visions. They let them fade. They lose them or deny them. Then they feel that they have never been given an opportunity.

So when we are given a vision, we must acknowledge it and ground it until it becomes reality.

My Indian friend and I then started to talk about miracles. She told me of a friend of hers who was a devotee of Baba Gee. This friend worked very hard caring for her family and was extremely tired. As she washed up a mountain of dishes one day, there was a flash of light and Baba Gee stood in front of her. He told her that he had noticed how hard she worked for others and had come to help her. He put on an apron and helped her with the dishes. When they were finished he told her he would come when she needed him, gave back the apron, smiled an understanding smile and disappeared. Now I call that a really practical miracle.

It reminded me of something which happened to a friend of mine, which I now shared with my companion.

My friend, who I will call Barry, had been working tremendously long hours to maintain his business. Night after night he drove home very late, hardly able to keep his eyes open. One night the inevitable happened. Just before he reached a major roundabout, busy with traffic, he fell asleep. He woke with a start on the far side of the roundabout.

An angel was sitting serenely beside him, its hands on the wheel. This angelic Being had negotiated the roundabout with all its traffic for him.

As soon as Barry was fully in command of his senses, the angel vanished, leaving Barry feeling awed, amazed and with an incredible sense of being protected. He still looked dazed when he told me the story next day.

In this way a memorable hour passed between an elderly Indian artist and a middle-aged European tourist, who had very little in common except the Universal language of miracles. Needless to say I bought her batik and have it hanging in my home to remind me of that afternoon.

What we give away comes back

The Universe is wonderfully economical with energy. If it can draw more than one lesson to our attention at a time it will.

When I first started working for myself I was not very well off. I had met a woman while I was training as a hypnotherapist. We became friends but I did not see her very often. I woke up one morning with a very strong impression that I had to send her money. I had not seen her for six months and I did not know what was wrong but just that I must do this.

I immediately wrote out a cheque for the amount I had in my bank account and sent it to her.

She contacted me the next day and said that she had been frantic for money. She had enough either to advertise for clients or to pay the rent. She could not do both. In fact she had been so desperate that she had gone to a clairvoyant who said to her, 'Don't worry, dear. There's money for your rent coming in the post.' My friend was very bemused. She could not think of anyone who would send her money. Then, out of the blue, my cheque arrived the next morning. It was the exact amount of her rent.

I did not think about the money again and saw my friend sporadically over the next few years. One evening I had an excited phone call from her. She wanted me to come to a party and I could make money! It sounded exciting and intriguing so I went. I had tremendous fun, bought a winning ticket and made a lot of money

It was years later before I realized that I had won exactly ten times the amount I had sent her!

We cannot give anything away with love for it will come back to us. When we give money away with love it comes back to us tenfold.

Out of darkness comes light

One time I had been overworking and had got out of balance. In response to my negative thoughts, everything was going badly. I did not want to get up but I forced myself out of bed. I did not feel like making my usual morning affirmation: *Today is a glorious day. Wonderful things are coming my way.* But I did. I made myself throw open my arms, make my affirmation aloud and smile. Because I did not want to do it, I repeated it aloud ten times.

As I made the affirmation, I remembered my daughter introducing me some months previously to a friend of hers. He was only a young man but he looked tense and careworn. She told me that his mother had gone into hospital that morning for an operation and the prognosis was bad, his girlfriend had left him and he could not get over it. To top it all he had just been made redundant.

A fortnight after I met her friend, I spoke to my daughter on the phone and she said, 'You remember the man I introduced you to? Well, his mother made a miraculous recovery and is out of hospital already. He's been offered a new job which is just what he wants. And he met a girl the day after you met him and he is in love.' In fact he married her six months later.

I went downstairs and there was a letter in the post asking me to do some workshops I really wanted to do. Then there was a phone call from an old friend. I felt great.

When we keep faith with the Light during the hours of darkness, then the Light must return.

When we are in tune with life

When we are in balance and walking on our Pathway, the brambles are cleared out of the way for us.

I told my literary agent that I would like *Transform Your Life* to be published by Piatkus who had a very good reputation for supporting their authors. She said that she would send the script to them.

Meanwhile Judy Piatkus, the head of the publishing house, went into a bookshop in London and asked them to recommend a metaphysical book and they suggested *Light Up Your Life*. She read and enjoyed it. Two weeks later she went into another bookshop and asked them to recommend a metaphysical book. They suggested *A Time for Transformation*. She went back to the office and said, 'I think the Universe is trying to tell me something.'

After she had read it, she said to her colleagues. 'I'd like to publish something of Diana Cooper's.' The script for *Transform Your Life* arrived on her desk that day! That is synchronicity.

When we listen to our intuition and act on it, seeming miracles happen.

A friend of mine wanted to get married on a particular Saturday in September. She and her fiancé listed the possible venues for the reception and toured round to look at them all. But they were all fully booked. The hotel they liked most had been booked up eighteen months beforehand for that date.

They were going away for a few days and set off in a slightly despondent mood. Two hours later they were motoring along a country lane and suddenly she had an intuitive flash. 'Please stop at the next phone box,' she said to her fiancé. 'I must phone Mum and ask her to go in person to that hotel as soon as possible.'

She phoned her mother from a call box in the next village. 'Please could you go down in person?' she asked. 'Phoning isn't good enough.'

Her mother trusted her daughter's intuition. She dropped what she was doing and jumped into the car. When she arrived at the hotel, the manager was still holding the phone in his hand. The long-standing booking for their date in September was just being cancelled. Someone else wanted that date but as she was there in person, he gave it to her.

Acting with integrity

If a child tries to steal out of our purse, we feel angry and punish him. If he asks nicely for what he wants we give it to him. The Universal energy is no different.

A client wanted to come on a one-week workshop. She did not have enough holiday from work and she told me that she was proposing to phone in sick so that she could do the course. What a way to earn karma!

I told her that I would be very happy for her to do the course but only if she did it with the highest integrity and certainly not by saying she was sick. However, I suggested that if she wanted to do the workshop she must tell the Universe and leave the *how* to them. If it was right they would bring it about for her.

Now this client worked for a firm run by computers. Soon after this she received a computer print out to say that she had five days leave owing to her. When she queried it she was told that the computer was never wrong. So when she acted honestly the Universe found a way for her to come on the course.

Working with crystals

Crystals absorb energies and transmute them. They also magnify energies and focus them. Each variety of crystal has its own particular type of energy, just as each medicinal herb heals a certain vibration of sickness. So a rose quartz vibrates with the heart centre and lapis lazuli with the third eye.

Muldovite is an extra-terrestrial meteorite which is energized to link the wearer to their Higher Self. This means it will help people to stay on their Pathway, not always the most comfortable experience if we have been dodging life's lessons!

Like all crystals it sometimes works in quite spectacular ways.

I had talked to my oldest daughter, Cheryl, about muldovite and its properties and she asked me to get her a piece. She had always been interested in the esoteric world. However her work and lifestyle left no time for her to develop her latent abilities. On her next visit I gave her the piece of muldovite I had bought her.

She had brought with her a friend who came from a very abusive home. They intended to spend one night at my house and then travel on to stay with the friend's family. The friend had not been home for some time and naturally she was feeling quite shaky as all the old memories started to surface.

When they arrived at her friend's home her Dad seemed reserved and not quite comfortable. But at least he was polite – apparently he was often downright rude to his daughter's visitors.

They ate dinner together but her Dad was excluded from the conversation. Then the family went for a walk. Cheryl asked her friend's father if he wanted to come too. He seemed pleased to be asked, but she got the impression he felt he wasn't wanted and he declined. She told me that she had never been in a family situation where she felt one person so set apart.

That evening when everyone had gone to bed, the two girls sat in the living room chatting. Cheryl felt a great surge of warm, tingly, pulsating energy flowing from her hands. She knew it was from the muldavite and she knew it was for her friend, so she asked her if she would like to receive it. Her friend said, 'Yes!' So Cheryl sat with her hands around her for a long time until the energy had gone.

My daughter later learnt that while she was receiving the energy, her friend started to feel differently about her

Dad. That night she slept deeply and woke seeing many things from her Dad's perspective. For the first time she could remember she felt understanding and loving towards him. From the next day there was an unmistakable change in her father. He was warm and friendly and went out of his way to take them to places and spend time with them. Something very important had healed.

Learn to activate miracles. Keep expecting them. They happen all the time.

CHAPTER 23

Peace Practice

The ancients used certain practices to attain and maintain inner peace. These included breathing techniques, yoga and exercise, colours, sounds, fun and good thinking, all of which calm and centre us.

When we are calm and centred our aura emanates a peaceful radiation which attracts harmonious people and conditions into our life.

Working with the breath

Our breath controls our mood and our mood affects our breathing. Everything is interdependent. When we feel anxious we breathe shallowly. Shallow breathing increases feelings of anxiety. Deep breathing induces calm and inner peace.

Anxiety states can effectively be interrupted and changed by altering our pattern of breathing.

For many of us, our first breath was taken in a hostile hospital environment of bright lights, noise, sterile colour, antiseptic smell and rigid shapes. Each one of these factors creates anxiety. So our first breaths may well have been shallow and frightened. We may even have been in shock. Indeed many of us never learn to use our full lung capacity.

Doing daily and regular breathing exercises can dramatically help us to let go of fears, phobias and tensions, which have robbed us of the inner peace which is our natural state.

Breathing Exercises

A very simple breathing exercise is to lie flat on the floor and focus on our base chakra. Breathe gently and rhythmically into this chakra to the count of four, then out to the count of four. Before long as this chakra begins to relax it will feel warm and may even become hot. We can do this simple breathing exercise into any chakra depending on where we hold tension but the base chakra is always a good place to start.

Another breathing exercise I find very effective is this. Sit comfortably, and imagine light coming down through our crown centre and into our heart. Then as we breathe in, we bring down light into the heart. As we breathe out we direct love into any part of the body that needs it. Concentrate on letting the love relax the muscles.

Lie or sit comfortably with your hands on your tummy. Breathe slowly in and out of your tummy so that it expands like a balloon. Do this four times. Then breathe slowly in and out of your lungs so that your rib cage expands. Do this four times. Breathe slowly in and out of your chest four times. Then fill up your tummy, rib cage and chest. Breathe out in reverse, chest, rib cage and tummy.

A very powerful breathing exercise which gets easier with practise is to sit comfortably with the spine straight. Breathe in to the count of four. Hold for the count of sixteen. Breathe out slowly to the count of eight.

The masters trained themselves to attain total calm, whatever the provocation, in three breaths.

Soothing with sound

Scientific research shows that discordant music can stultify the growth of plants while classical music promotes luxurious growth. Humans too are sensitive to sound. Most of us know that jangly sounds emit shock waves which can give us a headache or make us feel bad tempered and stressed.

The vibration of inharmonious sounds can ruffle or in extreme cases destroy our protective aura. Harmonious sounds can soothe and stroke our auras and make us feel good. Listening to beautiful music is a peace practice.

Harmony with colour

Each colour has its own vibration. Reds excite us. Oranges warm. Yellow promotes left brain thinking. Green, the colour of nature and of the heart centre, is a harmonious colour. Surrounded by the vibrations of green we automatically feel emotionally soothed. Blue, too, calms our brain waves. Deep shades of blue help to promote peace when we are mentally restless or disturbed. Violet is a higher spiritual colour which pacifies our soul.

We may not be able to walk in leafy green nature or to luxuriate by a cool blue pool or even indulge in a trip to blue skies or violet mountains but we can all visit these places in our thoughts and imaginations.

When we relax and imagine we are by a beautiful serene lake, with warm sun shining from a blue sky, our mind acts as if we are physically there and our body unwinds accordingly.

So by thinking of green nature, of blue skies and quiet waters we can find the path to peace.

Happy thoughts

Happiness makes us healthy just as good health makes us happy. Happiness is a result of right thinking. This means taking our thoughts on happy journeys. After all, a thought appears and we have a choice where we travel with it. We may travel with that thought down into the depths and embroider a dark picture for ourself, or we may fly with the thought to weave a joyous fantasy or we may lift that thought to God. Just where we journey with each thought creates our health and our future.

Our thoughts are seeds and we harvest what we sow and tend. When we sow and nurture seeds of serenity we harvest inner peace.

Our body is a chemical factory. These chemicals affect our moods and our moods manufacture chemicals. When we are depressed, doctors give us drugs which produce endorphins to change our chemistry and lift our mood. When we laugh our body produces the same endorphins which lighten our mood. Laughter is free and has no side effects.

Happiness practices are spiritual practices. Joyful laughter is a spiritual practice.

Meditation

Meditation harmonizes our brain waves. When the waves of the sea are calm, we have a peaceful day. When the waves of our brain are calm, we have a peaceful day.

Simple rules for meditation are: Sit in the same place at the same time for the same length of time each day. Habit is powerful. If we have a quiet corner where we meditate each day, at that time and place our brain waves will automatically quieten.

The purpose of meditation is to quieten the mind so that we can listen to God and there are many ways to do this. Some people take a mantra, which is a word or phrase, and repeat it again and again until their mind is quiet and they can let it go. Many people use or are given meaningless mantras. These open people up to any energy, not necessarily beneficial. In the temples the names of gods were chanted and this called in the quality which that god, who was seen as one aspect of Source, represented. Here are some examples:

Om namah shivaya	This mantra calls on shiva, the destroyer of illusion. To use this mantra we must be serious about our spiritual growth for it promotes an accelerated path, breaking down our inner fears and attracting to us situations which allow us to face these fears.
Om namo narayanaya	This mantra invokes a supportive, protective energy which balances us and brings us to inner peace.

Om mani padme hum	This means 'welcome to the thousand-petalled lotus' and dedicates us to the path of enlightenment.
Jesus Christ	This calls on the Christ consciousness which opens the heart centre.

Others prefer to watch the breath, focusing on a steady breath in and out, until the mind becomes quiet. Some like to focus their mind on a picture then close their eyes and hold the imprint of the picture in their inner vision. A candle is excellent. Look at a lighted candle for as long as possible, then close your eyes and continue to watch the candle.

Candles, music, incense, flowers, beautiful objects all help to raise the energy so that we can meditate at a higher level.

Meditation relaxes the body, quietens the brain waves, lowers the blood pressure and induces calm. These are a prerequisite of inner peace.

Spiritual practices are peace practices.

Stretching

When we are afraid, we tense up. *The purpose of tension is to draw our attention to something amiss*. There is divine wisdom held within every cell and if we contract that area of our body, we cannot access the divine wisdom.

Oxygen carries life force round our body. It cannot reach where we are in tension. So exercise and stretching can help to bring vital energy to these cut off areas. As the life returns, awareness surfaces.

Where joints are stiff, we have accumulated negative

224

emotions. Most of us resist change. If we are afraid to move forward our hips stiffen. If we feel burdened with problems, our shoulders ache.

Stretching, through yoga or exercise, frees us. When we free our hips, new ways of moving forward present themselves to us. When we rotate and strengthen our ankles our own confidence supports us. When we relax our shoulders new solutions to our problems are found. This is cosmic law.

My hips were very stiff and uncomfortable. I did not know what it was about or what I was resisting about moving forward in life. However, it was fairly obvious that I was resisting something. A friend showed me yoga postures to practise which would open up my hips and allow me the freedom to move forward.

What happened then was very uncomfortable and very releasing. As I did the exercises and my hips became free, I realized that my husband and I were no longer walking the same path. Not only that, I was going much faster than he was.

He was such a kind, loving and gentle man. Yet I knew that it no longer served my growth or his to walk with him. I must move on and let him walk his Pathway at his pace. Six months later, lovingly and caringly, though with much sadness, we had sold the house and started to walk our separate Paths.

Someone said to me. 'I think I would rather have stiff hips!' Of course that is a choice.

When we are tense we cannot be at peace. Free our tension, and we start our journey to peace.

STRETCHING EXERCISES

Starting our day with a few simple exercises can help our energies to flow and our body to feel vital and supple.

- Stretch both arms as high as possible.
- Stretch up one arm and turn it as if screwing in a light bulb. Repeat with the other arm.
- Gently drop the neck forward and rotate it in a circle to the right four times.
- Repeat in the opposite direction four times.
- Rotate your shoulders forward four times.
- Rotate your shoulders backwards four times.
- With your hands by your sides, gently lean to the right stretching down as far as possible.
- Repeat to the left.
- Put your hands on your hips and swivel to the right four times. Repeat to the left four times.
- Put your hands on your hips and bend to the right four times. Repeat to the left four times.
- Lift your right knee. Hold it with your hand and pull it up to your chest.
- Repeat with left knee.
- Swivel your hips in a circle to the right four times. Repeat to the left four times.
- Bend your knees and swivel in each direction four times.
- Stand or sit and rotate each ankle in turn four times.
- Sit on the floor. Bring your feet together at the groin and hold. Drop your knees to the floor in a butterfly movement and flap your wings.
- Lie on the floor with your feet flat on the floor and your knees raised. Drop your knees gently to the right.

Repeat to the left four times.
* Bring your right knee to your chest and hold. Repeat with your left knee. Repeat with both knees.

Healthy lifestyle

Healthy food builds healthy bodies. If we poisoned our dog, we would not expect it to be happy. Yet we poison our bodies with sugar, aspirin, alcohol and chemical fertilizers and expect to be happy.

Healthy foods make us happy.

Certain foods are hard to digest and may cause discomfort. Easy-to-digest foods result in peaceful stomachs.

Rhythmic walking or swimming, gentle exercise of any kind cleanses the body and frees it of toxins.

Doing something we enjoy doing and which gives us satisfaction promotes a happy mind. Singing, dancing, drumming and humming shake out the negative vibrations. Taking time off to play, have fun, pursue hobbies and have holidays ensures that we stay in balance. Allowing ourselves quality sleep time enables us to remain healthy and surrounding ourselves with like-minded, positive people raises our spirits.

Holding loving thoughts

Of all routes to inner peace, right thinking is the most important. So often we sabotage inner peace with a negative thought.

When we consciously let go of hurting, jealous, negative thoughts and focus on right thinking towards others, inner peace is assured.

227

When someone treats us badly or does us an injustice it is worth picturing them happy and their venture being successful. I know it is difficult. I have fought against it many times but we have a thousand fold reward in terms of inner peace. And we earn karmic brownie points.

Right thinking heals us in body, mind and spirit.

I find it helps me to set my mind each day. I start by welcoming the day with these words. 'I welcome this glorious day. Wonderful things are coming my way.' Then I stretch fully and as I reach up I say, 'Let my Higher Self take over today with Divine Intelligence in command.'

Deep in the centre of each of us is a pool of peace. When we connect with this space we can face our fears with equanimity, recognizing them as messengers. We can regain our confidence, our faith in ourself. We can listen to the quiet, still voice of our Higher Self.

CHAPTER 24

The Great Connection

An ocean is vast, yet any water taken from it, whatever it is used for, contains the energy of the ocean. Rain and rivers all return to the ocean.

The Divine Source is a great ocean of energy. Anything taken from it contains the energy of Source and all things return ultimately to Source. Every human, animal, plant or mineral is formed from the energy of the Divine Source and must return to merge with it. Whatever we do, we are permeated with this Divine energy.

I could never understand that we are all each other until I learnt about spiritual evolution.

Spiritual evolution

The mineral has a sleeping consciousness. It absorbs positive and negative energy quite impartially and radiates what it absorbs. And so it sleeps, evolving slowly over billions of years until it is sufficiently aroused to move on to a plant consciousness.

A plant feels but does not have emotions. It responds to different kinds of music, to hate or to love. It reacts to all our thoughts and tones of voice. Most plants are sensitive to atmosphere. When a person is in tune with plants they respond to him and she or he is known as having green fingers.

So if we intend to cut a plant, it is a cosmic courtesy mentally to ask it first. Then, prepared rather than shocked, it will offer itself with love to us. Plants are also learning about loving service.

We are here to serve nature not the other way round. We need nature which does not need us. When we humbly realize this, nature gladly offers to feed and nourish us. Then we absorb loving vibrations which keep us healthy.

The plant evolves until it is ready to experience an animal consciousness. At first it is a part of a group soul, such as the group soul of a flock of birds. Gradually it evolves to become an individual soul within a more highly developed animal.

Evolution moves us on to become a human soul and start the journey through lifetimes of growth to where we are now.

Within our cellular memory is the imprint of our mineral, vegetable and animal consciousness and experience. All things are literally within us and part of us. We cannot hurt a rock, a plant or an animal without hurting part of us and all that is.

However, when we act with good will, good intention and harmlessness, plants or animals will offer themselves to us (at least their Higher Self will). As they offer their lives to support us, they grow in consciousness.

Our consciousness is linked to ants and bees and mice and all creatures. If they are sharing our space and it feels inappropriate, we can link into their higher consciousness, communicate and ask them to move to a more suitable place. We should make sure that there is such a place for them. Communication does not pollute the Earth and it promotes love and trust between all species. They will usually move, being more flexible than we are. However if they do not and we decide to use other methods to move them on, we must tell them of our intention before we do it.

When we have a problem with a person, we do not put up barriers and shutters. We talk to their Higher Self lovingly in an effort to resolve matters in the highest possible way for all concerned. In the same way we can talk to the soul or group soul of the crystal, plant or animal. All this will help speed the process ahead, just as loving communication helps when we are open and receptive to the more highly evolved beings in the Spiritual planes.

Transformation on Earth

At present, as I have already mentioned, Planet Earth is a third-dimensional planet. We are in the process of making a meteoric transformation through the fourth dimension into a fifth-dimensional planet.

At the third dimension our reality is what we can see, hear and touch. We are unaware of anything beyond this. We live in a physical, material world only. Third dimensional beings tend to use the earth and resources of the planet as if there were no tomorrow and as if it is their right to do so. At this level we believe we are human beings who happen to be on this planet and that some people just may have occasional otherworldly experiences. This is often disparagingly called imagination.

As fourth dimensional beings we become aware of the spiritual dimensions. We are aware that we are spiritual beings in a body for a chosen opportunity on Earth. We know our essence is spirit and we have a desire to work with and for the Light.

As Light workers we aim to raise our vibrations constantly and consistently until we can bring a high voltage of Light through our chakras to the Earth and to other beings.

As the general energy of Planet Earth rises, people are becoming more psychically attuned. We are becoming more telepathic, clairvoyant and prophetic. We are more able to tune into each other and to the world around us, so we are able to offer more understanding, compassion and healing to each other. This is taking place now.

At the fifth dimension, we are superconscious beings. Because at this level we are attuned to the spiritual forces and know we are immensely powerful creators, we feel at peace. We only desire to serve the Light. Nothing else is of importance. We have incredible energies. *At the fifth dimension we take mastery and are co-creators with God. To serve the Light and have the clarity, wisdom and power to do so is a peaceful state of being.*

As fifth-dimensional beings we walk free and independent without need for the approval or agreement of others. Our security is within. We speak our Truth. Therefore we are incredibly powerful.

We are complete. We do not need a mate for support

or sustenance. If we meet a soul mate to walk our path with us for a while, that is a delight and a pleasure but we do not need to have it. We are equally at peace on our own.

At this level, attuned to the higher forces we manifest by our command.

We are beings without attachments and as such we have all that is of importance in the world.

At the third dimension we make change by impressing the subconscious with new beliefs. At the fifth dimension we transform by direct application to our Higher Self for the energy to change.

This is an application to the Higher Self simplified from Superconscious Techniques channelled from Alarius who is one of the discarnate spiritual beings impressing higher wisdom into the awareness of people on Earth at this time.

'Higher Self, please manifest with ease and grace, the energy to . . . . in the highest way, so that the power of this energy is now embodied in my life. I ask for the capacity to deal with what I have asked for. Make sure that I am prepared and ready in every way to accept this into my experience. So it is.'

This is so powerful that we must use it mindfully with love and faith. We can, for example, ask for the energy to develop inner peace, or greater wisdom, or the ability to follow our Path as well as more material things. Whatever we ask of our Higher Self with faith will inevitably be set in motion.

There are many now evolving who are multi-dimensional, who span the dimensions and are constantly growing in brightness and inner strength.

More old souls are being born now than at any other time in the history of the planet. Many are causing consternation in their families by refusing to eat meat or collude in the old dishonesties. But they bring the promise of great peace in the future.

The task of Light workers now is to prepare the way for the Illumined Ones or Star Birds who will incarnate in the next century to bring peace and light to our planet.

At this moment now gathered round Planet Earth are many Higher Beings. They are waiting for us to ask for help. There is so much assistance available to us from spirit, from ancestors and loved ones, from guides, helpers, avatars, angels, Buddha, Christ, God. *We have to ask*. They are so willing to help but cannot step in until we make the request so remember that *prayer is powerful*.

The energy of the Cosmic Christ is pouring through Planet Earth, touching minds that are open. This vast energy of Universal Love is sweeping away religious dogma so that we may all become spirits of the Universe. At this level we know that Love in the only religion. There is only Love.

And yet more exciting, uplifting, luminous energies are waiting to come in, sweeping us off our feet, confusing us, twirling our reality and leaving us purer, more aware and breathless with wonder at our new expanded perceptions. They will leave us with a profound sense of inner peace.

When we are at peace, we have within us incredible power to heal and change our world.